LOST FORTS OF CASPER

JOHANNA WICKMAN

FOREWORD BY DOUGLAS R. CUBBISON

THE History PRESS

Published by The History Press
Charleston, SC
www.historypress.net

Front cover image: author's collection.

First published 2016

Manufactured in the United States

ISBN 978.1.46711.922.1

Library of Congress Control Number: 2015958238

Notice: The information in this book is true and complete to the best of our knowledge. It is offered without guarantee on the part of the author or The History Press. The author and The History Press disclaim all liability in connection with the use of this book.

To my loving family and Pearl

CONTENTS

FOREWORD

Today, Casper is a quiet, prosperous community located nearly in the middle of Wyoming. It is the second-largest city in the state and is the center of the energy industry of Wyoming, which powers the nation. The North Platte River, which divides the community, is crossed by numerous modern bridges and was tamed by the construction of dams and reservoirs early in the twentieth century. Today, viewing the private vehicles, commercial trucks and oil rigs flowing through its streets and highways, it is difficult to envision the Casper of 150 years ago. Yet that Casper was at the middle of the great overland trails, and its crossings of the then turbulent and often violent North Platte River were key terrain along those trails.

From the earliest days of the Oregon and California Trails, the Bessemer Bend crossing of the North Platte, just west of modern Casper, was known as the last ford and ferry of the river. In 1852, a French trader and entrepreneur known as John Baptiste Richard constructed what would become known as Reshaw's Bridge east of modern Casper in what is today Evansville. Reshaw's Bridge (more properly known as Richard's Bridge) almost immediately became one of the most important locations along the overland trails. Another bridge constructed by a competitor, Louis Guinard, shortly followed several miles to the west. In 1860, a Pony Express station was established at Guinard's Bridge. In 1861, the Pacific and Overland Telegraph Companies constructed a transcontinental telegraph system linking California and the remainder of the nation, and they placed one of the string of telegraph stations at Guinard's Bridge. Such a critical location shortly attracted the attention of the U.S. Army, as it attempted to provide route security to the long and vulnerable line of communications and transportation extending through the territory of numerous hostile Indian nations. In the early years of the Civil War, the army would construct Platte Bridge Station to safeguard the telegraph station at Guinard's Bridge.

Understandably, the ensuing maelstrom of combat in late July 1865 at the Platte Bridge Station has garnered considerable attention. The courageous sacrifice of twenty-year-old Lieutenant Caspar Collins—leading a forlorn hope and desperately striving to relieve a wagon train being assailed by Sioux, Northern Cheyenne and Arapahoe warriors west of Guinard's Bridge—is a story as enthralling and thrilling, as passionate and poignant, as anything that our nation's storied heritage can offer.

Unfortunately, fifteen years of military activity around Bessemer's Bend, Richard's Bridge and Guinard's Bridge has been overshadowed by the momentous events of July 26, 1865. Johanna Wickman, who grew up in Casper, addresses these nearly forgotten army scouts, encampments, patrols and skirmishes.

The 1850s encampments garrisoning Richard's Bridge, particularly their role in the 1857–58 Mormon Rebellion, have garnered little interest from historians. Johanna provides the first comprehensive assessment of these camps, which is incredibly valuable since the archaeological remnants of the army's presence here were recently eradicated by residential development fostered by the government of the town of Evansville, Wyoming.

Camp Dodge, located along Garden Creek on the northern slopes of Casper Mountain, has long been discounted by local historians as comprising little more than a "lumber camp." Rather, Wickman's exhaustive research reveals Camp Dodge to have been a full regimental headquarters that had important influences on military operations along the North Platte for a substantial portion of 1865.

Other violent skirmishes—such as a major engagement that was fought on horseback extending for miles along Casper Creek on June 3, 1865—are also afforded coverage by Wickman's volume.

The full story of the army on the North Platte River, from Reshaw's Bridge to Bessemer Bend Crossing, for a decade and a half has remained sorely neglected for far too long. Johanna's treatise provides a laudable study of the full story of this integral aspect of Wyoming and national history.

DOUGLAS R. CUBBISON
Curator for the Wyoming Veterans Memorial Museum
Casper, Wyoming

PREFACE

This book is the result of many hours of research over two years, poring over countless original documents and even a trip to the National Archives in Washington, D.C. The impetus for this came through the need to research a local history topic for the completion of my master's degree through the University of Nebraska at Kearney. I chose this topic because of my nearly lifelong interest in the Civil War and historic preservation.

At the time I was required to choose my topic for the University of Nebraska, the site of Post at Platte Bridge had just been sold, and the location was to be bulldozed and turned into a housing development. As I began researching Post at Platte Bridge, I became more and more frustrated that the site has been lost despite its fascinating history. My hope is that this book will help to both educate and entertain so that critical historic sites like Post at Platte Bridge are not lost forever because people are unaware of their significance.

While researching this topic, I became fascinated by a number of characters, but the one who struck me the most is Colonel Preston B. Plumb. He is scarcely known in Casper, Wyoming, but his military service record here and throughout Wyoming was beyond reproach. Not only that, but he left behind an impressive résumé, including lawyer, statesman, newspaper editor/owner and U.S. senator. Did I mention he did half of those things prior to his military service in his early twenties? By all accounts, Plumb was a remarkable man, and I am glad to have discovered more about him through my research on this project.

I also discovered through this project that many of the other histories written on this topic tend to bash the Eleventh Kansas Cavalry quite a bit. I found that much of that was due to the bias of a single source, Lieutenant Bretney's son, which had permeated throughout the field. This book also aims to reclaim some of the reputation of the Eleventh Kansas that has been lost. The purpose is not to denigrate the Eleventh Ohio Cavalry in any way but, rather, to elevate the Eleventh Kansas Cavalry to the same level.

I hope that through reading this book you will come to love Casper's frontier military history as much as I have!

ACKNOWLEDGEMENTS

This book would not have been possible without the amazing support of my family. My parents, John and Martha, have continuously encouraged me throughout my life, and this was no exception. Mom helped me transcribe over one thousand original document pages I had photographed at the National Archives in Washington, D.C., and has been a critical editor of this document while it was being shaped for my master's thesis as well as this book. My sister Gloria also played an important role in helping me edit this document. Her writing expertise was invaluable. My other sister, Olivia, provided moral support and listened to these stories over and over as I became engrossed in my research. I also am indebted to my sweetheart, Tristan Birkemeier, for his support and help over the past few years. He accompanied me to the National Archives and helped me gather all the information that I needed.

Douglas Cubbison, friend and co-worker, provided me with many of the sources in this text through his own research trips and gave me considerable advice on the research and publication of this book. I would also like to thank John Goss for being so supportive and understanding when research and writing on this book took me away from the office. Bill Seid and Craig Lawson have my gratitude for letting me bounce ideas off them as my research progressed over the years.

Also, a big thank-you to the Fort Caspar Museum, Wyoming State Archives and the Kansas State Historical Society, which provided a wealth of research and many of the images seen in this book.

Acknowledgements

Finally, I would like to thank Artie Crisp and The History Press for working with me on this book and publishing all of my hard work. Thank you!

INTRODUCTION

Casper, Wyoming, is most famous to visitors and residents for its rich oil history. Yet Casper was the site of three major military outposts during the 1850s and 1860s. The most famous of these is Fort Caspar, a museum today. The written history of Fort Caspar often revolves around its namesake, Caspar Collins, and the Eleventh Ohio Volunteer Cavalry. This book includes a substantial amount of research on the Eleventh Kansas Volunteer Cavalry and its relationship with the Eleventh Ohio Volunteer Cavalry in order to create a more accurate representation of historical events at Fort Caspar. In addition, this study pays particular attention to Camp Dodge, regimental headquarters of the Eleventh Kansas, and Colonel Preston Plumb, neither of which has been heavily discussed in other titles. Lastly, original military records were consulted at the National Archives in Washington, D.C., in order to adequately ascertain the military's positions, orders and communications while in Casper.

All three of these posts appeared less significant than their larger counterparts, such as Fort Laramie. They had smaller garrisons and did not see the same number of dignitaries passing through. During the majority of its operation, Fort Caspar had only around one hundred men at the post. Camp Dodge fluctuated but likely never reached any numbers higher than that. Post at Platte Bridge never crossed one hundred men. Nevertheless, their purpose was just as important, albeit different from the larger forts. Post at Platte Bridge was established to protect a vital bridge crossing over the North Platte River. Later, it protected Albert Sidney Johnston's supply trains during the Mormon War. Post at Platte Bridge's purpose is heavily connected to the country's westward expansion and the perils that arose as so many Americans traveled across the frontier. In the case of Post at Platte Bridge, the army aided travelers and improved transportation in the area by securing a safe place for travelers to cross the river. In addition, Platte Bridge Station guarded the vital telegraph line connecting the populated East Coast with the newly developed West Coast. Platte Bridge Station also oversaw the smaller outposts of Sweetwater Station and South Pass (among others), which were tasked with relaying telegraph messages and maintaining the telegraph lines in their sector. This is in stark contrast to larger military outposts such as Fort Laramie, which began as a small trading post that was purchased by the military in 1849 and later grew into a major headquarters for the army during the Plains Indian Wars.[1] Though only around for approximately six weeks, Camp Dodge served as the regimental headquarters for the Eleventh Kansas Cavalry and was commanded by Colonel Preston Plumb.

Since the history of these three military outposts has become somewhat clouded through incomplete local history titles, it was best to consult as many primary sources as possible. To this end, the original military records of the Eleventh Kansas Volunteer Cavalry, Eleventh Ohio Volunteer Cavalry, letters to and from Fort Laramie and records of Post at Platte Bridge were all consulted at the National Archives in Washington, D.C. These provided invaluable firsthand accounts of Native American skirmishes, communications among the posts and Fort Laramie and reports of Native American incidents.

The first chapter of this study focuses on the first bridge crossings in the area and the establishment, operation and eventual closing of Post at Platte Bridge. It includes information on the post that has previously not been elaborated on, as well as information on the significance of the post's commanders that has not been discussed in other scholarly works.

The second chapter discusses the creation of Platte Bridge Station (Fort Caspar) and its position within the frontier. The chapter also illustrates how events that occurred far from the fort triggered hostilities that impacted the post. In addition, it includes a considerable amount of information on the Eleventh Kansas Volunteer Cavalry, Colonel Plumb and Camp Dodge, all of which are often glossed over or only minimally covered in scholarly works. This will also highlight the rivalry between the Eleventh Kansas and the Eleventh Ohio, the origins of it and how it impacted the operation of the post.

The last chapter describes the seminal Battle of Platte Bridge and the eventual closing of the fort. The death of Caspar Collins is also covered and includes perspectives from the Native American side that are often not featured in historical studies on the subject. It also discusses Major Martin Anderson's decision to send Caspar Collins on what was later regarded as a suicide mission and why he may have felt that it was a valid decision at the time.

This work seeks to provide a more complete and balanced picture of the Eleventh Kansas Cavalry and Eleventh Ohio Cavalry in the area by featuring previously neglected information on the Eleventh Kansas. This will help correct the reputation of the Eleventh Kansas and its service in this area. It also provides context and clarification for all three posts and their relationships with smaller outposts and Fort Laramie. In addition, it corrects some information that has been misrepresented in previous works. These three outposts played important roles in local and regional history. This book attempts to illustrate the history of Casper's three military outposts by focusing heavily on the original military records and diaries of those who were present at the posts. Through that, this book will prove that these three outposts are important to local and regional history.

Chapter 1

POST AT PLATTE BRIDGE

With the discovery of gold in faraway California, countless Americans braved the epic trek across the western wilderness for their chance at striking it rich. By the early 1850s, routes such as the Oregon Trail, Mormon Trail, California Trail and Overland Trail teemed with immigrants heading westward. The trip was perilous, and travelers faced inhospitable weather, disease, accidents and the occasional Native American attack. One of the most dangerous things for a pioneer in a covered wagon going west was crossing a river.

The Platte River was a force to be reckoned with during the mid-nineteenth century and was difficult to cross in the high water season. This situation, however, presented a fantastic opportunity for those skilled and entrepreneurial enough to set up bridge crossings along the river. The present-day city of Casper, Wyoming, encompasses a few of these crossings. Whenever they sprang up, traders set up nearby shops, which soon attracted the attention of local Native American tribes. These sites became hotbeds of activity as a result of having so many people concentrated in a single place. As is often the case with so many people in a small location, however, trouble broke out. Eventually, the military took notice and stepped in to control things. Its solution was to establish a permanent garrison of army personnel in the area to deal with any potential threats that might occur to travelers along the route. The Post at Platte Bridge became the first military presence in Casper and helped cement the area as a critical location to protect.

Travel on the Oregon Trail was often costly. Pictured are two graves along the trail from 1844 and 1845. *Wyoming State Archives, Department of State Parks and Cultural Resources.*

Although the most feared peril on the trails was Native American attacks, travelers were far more likely to die from disease, starvation or accidents. *Library of Congress.*

The first river crossing in the Casper area was organized by Brigham Young as his party of Mormons moved through the area on their way to Salt Lake City in 1847. They used a small skiff made of leather to ferry people's belongings back and forth across the river. The *Revenue Cutter*, as it was called, was eventually replaced by more durable rafts. Captain Howard Stansbury

Wagon crossings like these were often very perilous. Travelers much preferred crossing raging rivers by bridge if possible. *Library of Congress.*

of the Corps of Topographical Engineers—famous for creating the first topographical map of the Great Salt Lake—passed through the ferry site in 1849 and remarked on the community that developed around the crossing, which included a blacksmith shop and a couple of small outbuildings. The ferry operated during the high water season for six years before finally closing in 1852.[2] The standard crossing fee was $1.50 per wagon, which was a reasonable price at the time. The ferry operation also included a very profitable blacksmith shop for wagon repairs and any other needs that the settlers may have had.[3]

In 1852, the Mormon Ferry operation faced its first major competition: a crossing named Richard's Bridge. John Baptiste Richard (Re-Shar) was a well-known French trader and entrepreneur in the area, and he had already built successful trading posts and bridge crossings elsewhere. Richard chose a site in present-day Evansville, Wyoming, to build his bridge across the North Platte River. Richard's Bridge was a marvel of engineering. It stood 835 feet in length, 18 feet wide and 10 feet above the waterline. The bridge was constructed of cedar from Casper Mountain (approximately six miles away) and supported by twenty-three pylons of wood filled with large stones.

Pipe smoking was common in the nineteenth century. Soldiers and travelers would have had clay pipe heads similar to this one. This one originally included the full head of a king, but it has been broken. *Author's collection.*

Reportedly, the bridge cost a staggering $14,000.[4] It opened during the high water season of 1853 and quickly became one of the most popular places to cross the North Platte River. Richard charged $5 per wagon and $4 for every hundred head of cattle to cross his bridge.[5] By the summer of 1853, Richard is reported to have made over $40,000 in toll fees alone.[6] As a noted Native American trader, John Richard soon attracted the attention of local tribes, and the site became a bustling trading location. Richard also had his own blacksmith shop and store in order to fulfill the needs of the many pioneers passing through. Soon, commanders at Fort Laramie decided that it would be unwise to leave such a major bottleneck of pioneer travel unprotected.

In 1854, tensions on the trails near Fort Laramie increased after what came to be known as the Grattan Massacre. That summer, a group of Danish immigrants who had just converted to Mormonism traveled by Fort Laramie on their way to Utah. One of their cows, which was lame, straggled and separated from the herd and wandered into a Brule Sioux village. A visiting Miniconjou Sioux spotted the cow, slaughtered it and held a feast for the village. Once the immigrants arrived at Fort Laramie, they demanded that the military do something about the slaughtered cow. Lieutenant Fleming was hesitant to become involved in the affair because of the terms of the most recent peace treaty with the Sioux. This treaty stated that matters of this nature needed to be settled by the tribes rather than the military. A recent West Point graduate under Lieutenant Fleming's command named Lieutenant John Grattan, however, was eager to prove himself in the West. He convinced the lieutenant to let him go down to the Sioux village to settle things.[7]

Instead of taking ten men, as Fleming had suggested, Grattan approached the village with twenty-nine men and two howitzers. At first, Grattan's discussion with the Brule Sioux chief, Conquering Bear, was quite civilized.

Conquering Bear explained that since the warrior who stole the cow was a Miniconjou, he had no authority over him as a Brule chief. To smooth things over, he offered the Mormon traveler his choice of any one of his fine horses. Given the situation, this was a very generous offer. Grattan, however, angrily refused. Conquering Bear told Grattan and his men through their interpreter that since they had eaten the cow they could not return it, and if he would not accept a horse in exchange then they had nothing more to discuss. As Conquering Bear walked away, Grattan tried to intimidate him by ordering the men to move the howitzers into position as if to fire on the village. In the confusion, one of the soldiers opened fire. The shot hit Conquering Bear in the back and killed him. Enraged over the death of their chief, the twelve hundred warriors in the village quickly retaliated against Grattan and his men. Twenty-nine soldiers were killed at the scene. The final member of the group only lived long enough to reach Fort Laramie before dying of his wounds.[8]

The Grattan Massacre, as it came to be known, sent shockwaves reverberating throughout the West as tensions between the army and Plains tribes increased. The shaky peace they had enjoyed before the massacre was gone. Thirty men and a well-respected Sioux chief lay dead because of a lame cow. As a result, the military felt that it would be gross negligence on its part to leave this area of travel unprotected. Richard's Bridge served as a major crossing point for travelers, and their safety remained crucial. The commanding officer of Fort Laramie at the time, Major William Hoffman, recommended to his superior officer, General Harney, that he send a detachment of soldiers to Richard's Bridge for the protection of travelers and traders.[9] Hoffman, in a letter dated October 10, 1856, wrote, "It would be a cause of much embarrassment to persons traveling this route, and in times of high water would stop all trains and the mails, if this bridge over the Platte should be destroyed."[10]

In November 1855, a small military outpost was established at the site called Post at Platte Bridge. Although many civilians continued to refer to the bridge as Richard's Bridge, members of the military called the crossing the Post at Platte Bridge. This outpost itself, only in operation between 1855 and 1856, was sometimes referred to as Camp Davis. The first garrison of soldiers at the post was Lieutenant Deshler of the Tenth U.S. Infantry and twenty-five men. His orders from Major Hoffman were as follows: "When you arrive at the Bridge you will keep your party at all times on the alert, exercise day and night the greatest vigilance. It will parade under arms for inspection every evening at Sunset. During the night the Sentinels will call the half hours."[11]

This drawing illustrates the interior of an officer's tent and would be similar to the Sibley tents at Post at Platte Bridge. *Library of Congress.*

During this time, Richard, along with all the other white traders in the area, reported to Fort Laramie while General Harney began his campaign of vengeance against the tribes for the Grattan Massacre. As a result, when the first detachment of troops arrived at Richard's Bridge, Richard himself was not there. He was given the chance to return to his operation in December provided that he did not do business with any tribes. Richard, being married to an Oglala Sioux, outright refused and spent the winter of 1855 at Fort Laramie.[12]

Commanders at the Post at Platte Bridge rotated out on an almost monthly basis. By January 1856, Second Lieutenant Robert Clinton Hill of the Sixth U.S. Infantry had replaced Second Lieutenant John Mendenhall of the Fourth U.S. Artillery at the post.[13] In a span of only three months, the post went through three commanders, all of whom were West Point graduates. The military's monthly return for January lists the post as "Fort Clay," one of only a few mentions of that name.[14] The vast majority of military correspondence refers to it instead as the Post at Platte Bridge.

During this time, tensions between the U.S. government and Plains Indian tribes remained rocky at best. The Indian agent for the area, a man named

Thomas Twiss, had several disagreements with the military, and there was certainly no love lost between them. Born in 1803, Twiss graduated second in his class at West Point in 1826. He was then commissioned as a brevet second lieutenant in the U.S. Army Corps of Engineers and worked as a professor in philosophy at West Point before moving to South Carolina College in 1829 to teach mathematics, philosophy and astronomy. After eighteen years of teaching followed by six years working in the iron industry, Twiss accepted an appointment as an Indian agent for the Upper Platte Agency based out of Fort Laramie. Soon after, Twiss married an Oglala Sioux woman and fathered six children. According to John D. McDermott, author of *Frontier Crossroads: The History of Fort Caspar and the Upper Platte Crossing*, "His personal view of his charges was that they were 'rude, unpolished Barbarians, but nevertheless possessed many sterling virtues.'"[15]

One of the first disagreements between Twiss and the military at the Post at Platte Bridge occurred in March 1856. A band of Crow approached Lieutenant Hill requesting gunpowder for hunting game. Hill informed them that he had none to trade. The Crows left and returned a short time later with all the gunpowder that they requested. When asked where they found the supply, they replied that they had traded with Indian agent Thomas Twiss. Twiss, however, was under orders not to trade with any tribes until a peace treaty had been signed between the tribes and the U.S. government. News of this trade reached Major Hoffman at Fort Laramie, who was outraged that Twiss had breached these orders. He was ordered by Hoffman to immediately report to Fort Laramie and to cease all negotiations with Sioux bands. Twiss snarkily responded that he would observe the major's request to stop speaking with local tribes, but that if Hoffman wanted him to report to Fort Laramie, he would have to be taken there at gunpoint.[16] This dialogue proved typical of the rocky relationship between Twiss and Major Hoffman.

Accompanied by Captain Henry Heth, Company E of the Tenth U.S. Infantry, Richard finally returned to his bridge and trading post in March 1856.[17] A topic not well known involves the significance of the soldiers either stationed at the post or who frequently worked with it. During the Civil War, Heth gained notoriety as the Confederate general who famously engaged General John Buford's First Cavalry Division, mistook it for militia and triggered the three-day Battle of Gettysburg in 1863. Other Confederate generals present at the Battle of Gettysburg with ties to the Post at Platte Bridge included Dick Garnett, commander of Fort Laramie; and Lewis Armistead, also stationed at Fort Laramie. Armistead also made occasional visits to smaller outposts such as Post at Platte Bridge.

Henry Heth in his Confederate uniform, taken during the Civil War. *Library of Congress.*

Captain Heth arrived at the Post at Platte Bridge with a full company of men: three officers, three noncommissioned officers, a bugler and forty-six privates.[18] During Heth's time at the outpost, it was also known in some official military correspondence as "Camp Davis." The moniker Post at Platte Bridge, however, remained in constant use throughout its operation.

Not long after Heth's arrival, the first major incident took place at the post. The bridge was a very popular crossing point on the Platte River. As such, several Native American tribes found it a suitable location to build lodges and trade with the settlers as they passed through. By April 1856, the Cheyenne had roughly twenty lodges at the post. Charles Antoine, an employee of John Richard, also lived at Richard's Bridge. A Cheyenne warrior found four stray horses belonging to Antoine and decided to keep them. Outraged, Antoine approached Captain Heth to settle the matter. Heth instructed the Cheyenne warrior to return the horses to Antoine, as they did not belong to him. In exchange, Heth would provide him with five dollars per head in goods from the trading post. The Cheyenne accepted the offer and promised to bring the horses back to the post in the morning. Upon further thought that evening, however, he decided to return only three of the horses and keep the best one for himself. The warrior also added that he would shoot anyone who dared to take the horse from him. After hearing this, Heth ordered Lieutenant Nathan Dudley and thirty-five men to reclaim the goods given to the Cheyenne warrior, confiscate the horse and capture him. Lieutenant Dudley successfully completed his mission aside from the fact that the Cheyenne in question escaped his custody. The warrior, however, was wounded in the process. Lieutenant Dudley reported back to Heth at approximately 8:00 p.m. and was subsequently ordered to return to the Cheyenne lodges and take two men hostage. The following morning, Heth released one of the prisoners but kept the Cheyenne warrior Fire Wolf in irons in Richard's blacksmith shop. The freed prisoner was instructed to bring the fugitive Cheyenne back to the post, but if he could not be located, then he was to bring the man's father. Soon after releasing the prisoner, however, Heth discovered that the man in question and his father retaliated against the army by murdering and mutilating Peter Garnier. Garnier had been on his way to the bridge from Richard's grazing pasture.[19]

Captain Heth reported the incident to General Harney, who wished to have the whole affair settled at a conference at Fort Laramie. On May 17, 1856, Chief Dull Knife of the Cheyenne visited the fort and promised Major Hoffman that he would deliver the murderers to Fort Laramie. Hoffman warned the chief that if he did not meet his end of the promise all Cheyenne

A photograph of Fort Laramie taken in 1858. *Wyoming State Archives, Department of State Parks and Cultural Resources.*

would be considered enemies of the U.S. government. Unfortunately, Dull Knife did not keep his promise, and this matter combined with other incidents grew into a bloody campaign led by Colonel Sumner against the Cheyenne the following summer.[20]

Following this incident, Captain Heth found it necessary to request that the post be issued a mountain howitzer. At first the request was denied, but Major Hoffman later approved the howitzer after Heth resubmitted his request to the proper personnel.[21] Major Hoffman forwarded the request to his superior but did not fully see the need for the howitzer, writing, "Tho' I differ much with the Captain as to the necessity, on his urging it in two letters, and the possibility that it may give confidence to his command, and as it can well be spared from this post and there being an escort here to take charge of it, I thought it advisable to let him have it." Further correspondence suggests that it was Heth's intention to use the howitzer to arm one of his three blockhouses at the post.[22] Despite the incident being settled at Fort Laramie, Fire Wolf remained a prisoner

Square nails such as these would have been manufactured in the blacksmith's shop at Post at Platte Bridge. *Author's collection.*

in Richard's blacksmith shop. He stayed there until the closing of the post that fall.[23]

In July 1856, Lieutenant William Carlin and Company D of the Sixth U.S. Infantry replaced Captain Heth and Company E of the Tenth U.S. Infantry. The command structure of the post also changed in that it now reported directly to Fort Laramie as opposed to General Harney of the Sioux Expedition. A main reason for this change involved the fact that the Post at Platte Bridge was incredibly isolated and lacked the necessary structures for adequate food and supply storage. Realizing this, Major Hoffman determined that it would be more efficient to time the changing of troops at the post with the arrival of new supplies as opposed to sending fresh supplies more often. In other words, new detachments of troops would arrive with their own provisions, thus eliminating the need to send supply wagons through dangerous weather to the post.[24]

On August 24, 1856, the post received its final commander and detachment. Captain Charles S. Lovell, Company B, Sixth U.S. Infantry, relieved Lieutenant Carlin and Company D. Lovell's company consisted of

This large chunk of red ochre would have been used by Native Americans for trade. Smaller pieces could be broken off and sold or used to dye a variety of materials. *Author's collection.*

only forty-eight men. Soon after taking command, Lovell reported to Major Hoffman that between four hundred and five hundred Shoshoni and Crow came to the post wishing to trade horses with the white settlers in the area. These natives complained that there were not sufficient buffalo for them to hunt and trade, so they had hoped to trade with the settlers in a desperate act of securing goods.[25]

By the fall of 1856, Major Hoffman began to see the Post at Platte Bridge as more of a liability than anything else. Rotating troops out every couple of months proved too perilous in the winter months, and supplying the post during the winter was also incredibly difficult. On October 16, 1856, Cheyenne leaders met with Indian agent Thomas Twiss and signed a treaty promising to keep the peace. This news, combined with the perils of staffing the post in the winter months, led to Hoffman's decision to close and abandon the post in November 1856. On November 3, Lovell received orders to abandon the post as soon as possible and to return with his detachment to Fort Laramie. He was also to ask Richard and the other traders to watch and maintain the military's three huts at the post should there be any need for future use of them.[26] Once they abandoned the post, the Cheyenne prisoner Fire Wolf was transferred to Fort Laramie, resulting in his loss in the bureaucracy of the U.S. military. Numerous letters show Major Hoffman writing to his superiors in Washington, D.C., requesting instructions as to what to do with the prisoner. Unfortunately, Fire Wolf died of disease in April 1857 before the issue was ever resolved.[27]

The year 1857 proved to be a good one for John Richard. He diversified his business and branched out into gold mining after the discovery of gold on Pikes Peak in Colorado. He continued to operate the bridge on the Platte River and made considerable money selling livestock to Colonel Albert Sidney Johnston's Utah Expedition. Faced with an increasing number of conflicts between the Mormon settlers and the U.S. government and territorial officials, the U.S. military created the Utah Expedition. President Buchanan feared the Theodemocracy that was taking shape in the Utah Territory. Tension between the Mormon Church and federal government existed for nearly ten years before the Mormons began their exodus to Utah in 1847. By 1857, the federal government feared that the territory would plunge into open rebellion. The causes of the Utah Expedition, or "Mormon War," are still hotly debated today although the federal government's paranoia of a culture that it did not fully understand is often given as one cause. To remedy this situation, President Buchanan sent Albert Sidney Johnston and about 2,500 men from Kansas to the Utah Territory. Their route took them directly through Richard's Bridge and the abandoned Post at Platte Bridge. The Utah Expedition included several engagements fought with Mormons but no major battles. Mormon vigilantes frequently attacked wagon trains and used guerrilla warfare tactics to disrupt Johnston's supply lines. Civilian travelers paid the highest price for the conflict, as these vigilantes massacred many of them along the frontier trails. Over 120 men, women and children were killed at the Mountain Meadows Massacre in southern Utah; 17 children under the age of eight survived, as the Mormon attackers did not murder those young enough to convert to Mormonism.[28] Several other such murders occurred during this time but none as despicable as the Mountain Meadows Massacre. Fort Laramie's commanding officer, Major Hoffman, worried that bands of Mormons would attack the bridge in an effort to disrupt the supply line, so he once again opened the Post at Platte Bridge in July 1858.[29]

No longer just a post to protect travelers along the trails, the men at the Post at Platte Bridge worked to protect the supply lines to Johnston's Utah Expedition. The post now served as a military outpost protecting military personnel and supplies traveling between Fort Laramie and Johnston's army

Post at Platte Bridge suddenly became necessary to the army in 1858 in order to protect Albert Sidney Johnston's supply train. *Library of Congress.*

on the move to Utah. The garrison of the post consisted of Captain Joseph Roberts and Companies D and E of the Fourth U.S. Artillery. The journey to Richard's Bridge, which started at Fort Laramie on June 3, took an entire month, with the garrison arriving on July 3. During this second operation with Captain Roberts in command, the post was occasionally referred to as "Camp Payne" in military documents. The name "Post at Platte Bridge" continued to be used throughout its lifetime. Captain Roberts was accompanied at the post by seventy-nine men, including eight officers and seventy-one enlisted men. The post also had twenty-four civilian teamsters in its employ. The number of these teamsters varied throughout the seasons, with more being on hand during the warmer months. During the winter, travel along the route dramatically dropped off, and at times there were only three or four teamsters present at the site. The second opening of the post lasted approximately ten months, during which Captain Roberts and the Fourth U.S. Artillery remained in command.[30]

While Captain Roberts was in transit to the post in June 1858, the Mormon War came to an end. Brigham Young received a full pardon that June, almost a month before Roberts and his men arrived at the location. With the Utah Expedition coming to a close, Roberts's initial reason for occupying

Albert Sidney Johnston. *Library of Congress.*

the post was essentially gone before he even arrived. The government saw no further need for a military presence at the site shortly afterward. The same issues that had plagued the location during its first operation, however, remained. Supplying the post during the snowy season proved treacherous,

Bottles such as these would have been a common sight around the post. They were used for various wines, whiskeys and liqueurs. *Author's collection.*

and the weather continually plagued those stationed there. A letter sent to Fort Laramie on April 4, 1859, from Sergeant H. Ford on his way to the Post at Platte Bridge describes the dangers faced by the men at the outpost. He wrote, "I have the honor to report myself lying hear [*sic*] having been taken snow blind on the 30th Ult on my route to Platt [*sic*] Bridge, for three days I was in the mountains not knowing ware [*sic*] I was going, finaly [*sic*] an Indian who was out hunting found me about ten miles from this place, and came in to the station and got a party of men to bring me in were [*sic*] I am now stopping."[31]

Food at the post consisted of any local animals that they could hunt or trade for, such as buffalo and deer. They also received shipments of canned pigeons, calves' tongues, fresh salmon, sardines, sweetmeats and lobsters. In addition, the men received various liquors, candies, spices and other supplies with which to cook.[32] It is likely that they also hunted the locally plentiful antelope, although the post's previous commander, Henry Heth, did not care for the taste of it. In his account, he wrote, "The [antelope] flesh was not edible, it tasted exactly like chewing sage brush. We tried every conceivable way, boiled, roasted, corned, in stews, highly seasoned, but there was no way of disguising the powerful flavor of the sage."[33] As terrible as the food may have been, soldiers at the post also had to worry about their fellow soldiers.

Pronghorn antelope are still hunted around Wyoming today, but Henry Heth and his troops were not fond of their taste. *Library of Congress.*

While away from the post for several weeks during January 1859, two men of the Fourth U.S. Artillery broke into Captain Roberts's quarters and stole between $500 and $600 from his trunk. The two men were caught and imprisoned until Roberts's return, when a court-martial could be held. The first man, Private William Griffith of Company D, was found guilty of the crime and sentenced to forfeit all pay and allowances due him "save the just dues of the laundress and such fatigue clothing as may be necessary; to be indelibly marked on the right hip with the letter 'T' one inch and a half long; to be confined at hard labor in charge of the guard wearing shackles attached to both of his ankles, connected to a chain 2 feet long for eight (8) calendar months, and at the expiration of that period to be drummed out of service."[34] The second man, Private John Moke of Company D, was given the same sentence.

On March 23, 1859, the government issued an order to abandon the Post at Platte Bridge. The troops were to return to Fort Laramie with the supplies from the post, as well as any salvageable building materials.[35] The order reached Captain Roberts on April 13, 1859. His response to his superior officers the next day requested information on how to properly dispose of the buildings and supplies.

This letter gives the best description of what sort of buildings were at the site and the size of the post. He wrote that fifteen wagons would be needed to haul supplies back to Fort Laramie, with an additional ten wagons for the sick, medical supplies and the two companies at the post. He also suggested ten more wagons to take the building materials back to Fort Laramie. He wrote, "I would respectfully request instructions respecting the disposition to be made of the material used in the construction of the bunks, doors, windows etc. of the several buildings." This is especially significant as it remains the only official description of the physical appearance of the post. When the Post at Platte Bridge was originally inhabited between 1855 and 1856, it only included a maximum of three outbuildings, and the men were forced to sleep in Sibley tents. Captain Roberts's letter, however, clearly mentions "several" buildings at the post. He also notes that bunks needed to be moved, suggesting that the men were living in sturdier barracks rather than Sibley tents.[36] Travelers passing through the area also wrote about seeing "fifteen or twenty comfortable log houses" near the bridge and post.[37]

The only major event that occurred at the post during this time happened just as Captain Roberts and his garrison prepared to abandon the post. A Frenchman named LaBeau was fatally stabbed on April 26, 1859. The incident was reportedly caused by a Native American, and the officer of the day at the post made a concerted search for the assailant in the surrounding lodges. The culprit, however, was never found.[38]

By May 1, 1859, Captain Roberts and his command had left the Post at Platte Bridge and returned to Fort Laramie. Joseph Roberts would later go on to fame during the Civil War for writing the U.S. Army's comprehensive artillery manual. Richard's bridge crossing remained financially successful until Louis Guinard opened a competing bridge across the Platte about ten miles upriver. Guinard's Bridge soon put Richard's out of business and gave the army a new reason for a military presence in the vicinity of Casper.[39] John Richard, who opened the bridge crossing and lucrative trading post that turned the area into a hot spot of Native American and civilian traffic, died in 1875. While trading with the Sioux near Fort Laramie, he was camped in the snow between Fort Laramie and Fort Robinson. Two men, Joe Milner and Tom Newcomb, stopped and visited Richard and his companion, Alfred Pallardie. No one knows for sure what happened during that visit other than the fact that both Richard and Pallardie were murdered. Blame shifted between Milner and Newcomb. Due to a lack of evidence, however, neither was ever convicted. Eventually, the blame passed to a band of Cheyenne.[40]

The Post at Platte Bridge was first established to protect travelers along the overland trails from Native American attacks. During its initial operation from November 1855 to November 1856, it successfully protected Richard's Bridge crossing and attempted to settle any disputes between travelers and the Sioux and Cheyenne tribes camped nearby. What happened to Fire Wolf remains a tragic story to this day but also a perfect example of the military's strategy in Native American relations at that time. Thomas Twiss may have been more successful as the region's Indian agent if he had spent more time working with the Native Americans and the military rather than just creating confusion and disobeying orders from Fort Laramie. Twiss was a bit of a loose cannon, but he also held a great deal of experience in Sioux culture. This experience may have been put to greater use if he had been able to get along with Major Hoffman. Still, Major Hoffman wielded the most influence over the post through his actions at Fort Laramie.

Whatever events happened at Fort Laramie or in the region had an effect on the Post at Platte Bridge. Major Hoffman's attempt to settle the horse theft and subsequent murder of Peter Garnier plunged the entire area into conflict with the Cheyenne. No doubt the murderer needed to be caught, but declaring war on an entire tribe if he was not surrendered proved rather extreme. This affair throws into light the fact that many of the military's best and brightest lacked the training for dealing with Native Americans. Hoffman, Heth and the rest of the commanders of Platte Bridge were all West Point graduates. As such, they had received the best military training available and by all accounts were very bright men. In the matter of Native American relations, however, they were ignorant at best. All of these men came from homes back east, thus proving unfamiliar with the area and the

Members of the peace commission standing with Peter Richard and his wife (couple to the right of the horse) at Fort Laramie. *Wyoming State Archives, Department of State Parks and Cultural Resources.*

cultures of the tribes who lived there. Some came to the post already hating the Native Americans for crimes reported in the papers. Others simply did not understand native culture.

Lieutenant Grattan triggered a bloody campaign of retribution against the Sioux for the way he handled a stolen lame cow. Just like the others, Grattan received a West Point education but had no experience in dealing with the Cheyenne or the Sioux. He also did not understand the relationships between the smaller tribes of Sioux. His bravado resulted in his death and the deaths of all his men, along with enraging an army that simply saw the event as the murder of their brothers in arms that needed to be avenged.

This troubled relationship between the army and the Native Americans continued for many years, and the Casper area was certainly not exempt. Seesawing between peace treaties and retaliation killings, frontier Wyoming remained an unsafe place for the trail traveler and even worse for any man in an army uniform.

The Post at Platte Bridge fulfilled its mission and no longer served a purpose to the army after 1859. Traffic on the trails was heaviest only for

Left: Wooden telegraph insulator, exterior view, 1860s. *Wyoming State Archives, Department of State Parks and Cultural Resources.*

Right: Cutaway of a wooden telegraph insulator, 1860s. *Wyoming State Archives, Department of State Parks and Cultural Resources.*

about six weeks in the summer, leaving little for the garrison to do the rest of the year. The area sprang back to life, however, with the installation of the telegraph at Guinard's Bridge only a few miles upstream. Rather than protecting travelers or supply trains, the army was tasked with protecting hundreds of miles of telegraph wire from marauding Native Americans.

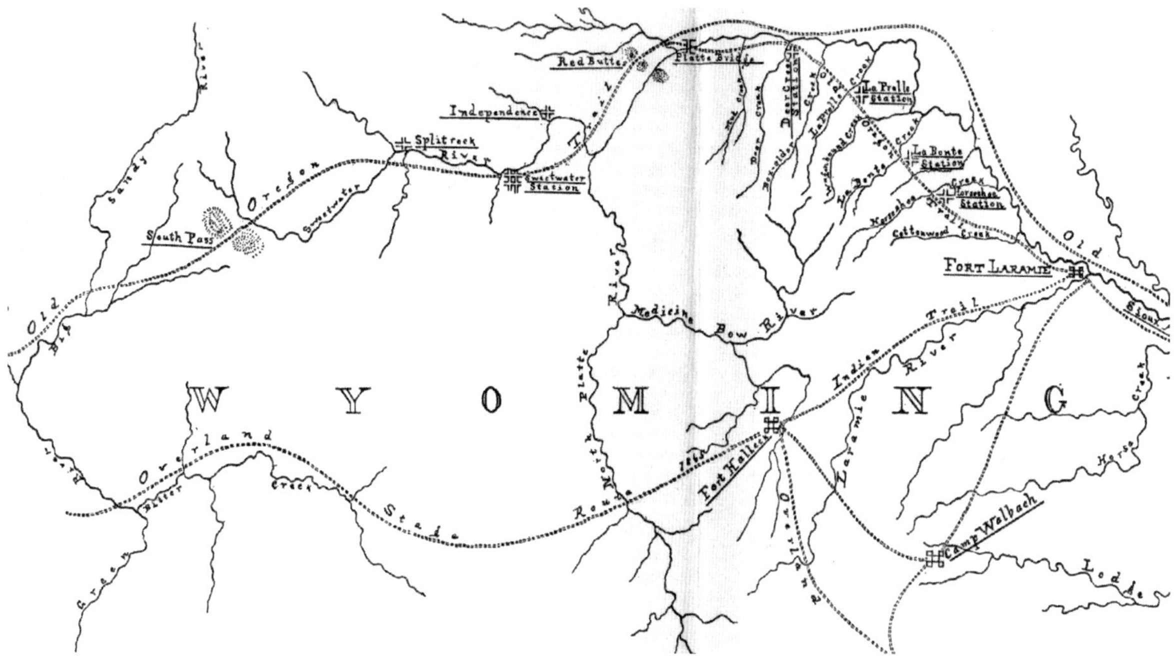

This map illustrates the location of Platte Bridge Station in relation to the other smaller telegraph outposts and Fort Laramie. Camp Dodge was located about five miles to the southwest of Platte Bridge Station. *William Elsey Connelley.*

Chapter 2

CONSTRUCTION OF PLATTE BRIDGE STATION, CAMP DODGE AND ESCALATION OF VIOLENCE

By 1859, John Richard no longer owned the only bridge crossing over the Platte River in the Casper area. A French-Canadian, Louis Guinard, opened his own bridge about ten miles upstream from Richard's. Guinard's Bridge was approximately 1,035 feet long, 18 feet wide and built from braced wood and iron in twenty-eight piers. Traffic at Guinard's Bridge soon eclipsed that at Richard's thanks in part to the telegraph station located at Guinard's crossing and Pony Express riders who chose to cross over the Platte through Guinard's Bridge.[41]

In August 1860, prolific British explorer Sir Richard Burton had the fortune to visit both bridge crossings and chronicled what he saw in his journals. He described the site of the army's Post at Platte Bridge with virtually nothing left. Only remnants of walls and broken floorings remained.[42] Later that afternoon, Burton arrived at Guinard's Bridge and gave a clear account of his experience there. He reported that the usual toll was $0.50 but that Guinard often charged Mormon trains $5.00 or more. According to Burton, the bridge was built at a cost of $40,000, which would equate to roughly $1.1 million in 2014 currency.[43]

The completion of the transcontinental telegraph line in 1861 rendered the Pony Express largely obsolete. Guinard's crossing had been chosen to house a telegraph station, which made it much more attractive to settlers passing through. Although the California gold rush had long since been over by 1860, traffic on the trails remained fairly high: "Fifteen thousand in 1860.

The Pony Express used Platte Bridge Station as a stop but was quickly outpaced by the new transcontinental telegraph system. *Library of Congress.*

Five thousand in 1861, five thousand in 1862, ten thousand in 1863, twenty thousand in 1864, twenty-five thousand in 1865 and twenty-five thousand in 1866."[44] As the location grew in popularity, it was forced to deal with the fact that it needed military protection. Local tribes were at first tolerant of Guinard's operation, but the situation soon became hostile after the death of his son.

Like Richard, Guinard had married into a local tribe, but unfortunately, that marriage did not spare him or his bridge crossing from Native American violence. The trouble began on October 4, 1860, when a war party of Unkpapa and Sans Arc Sioux came upon three white men within eight miles of the Upper Platte Agency at Deer Creek. First professing friendship, the warriors rode ahead and prepared an ambush. Discovering their plans, the men fled, but not before the Sioux put two arrows in the back of one of the men, a recently discharged soldier, who died the next day. On October 5, the raiders ran off four of Richard's horses and headed west, there to encounter Louis Guinard's son not far from Red Buttes. The boy had been sent out to herd horses, and it was his misfortune to run into the marauders. They killed him with arrows, leaving his cut and mangled body on the plains.[45]

In March 1861, the area now known as Wyoming became a part of the Dakota Territory as opposed to the Nebraska Territory, which it had been prior. This change did not affect much in the way of day-to-day life for those in the area. The transcontinental telegraph line had been a common target for sabotage and vandalism almost since its inception. Due to the range of the batteries used to power the lines, telegraph stations were needed approximately every seventy-five to one hundred miles. In 1862, the government began sending small detachments of soldiers to each of these stations to serve as guards and repairmen for the inevitable cut lines.

During the spring of 1862, the Shoshoni were the first to begin attacking the telegraph lines and stations across the region. An appeal to the War Department for better security on the route resulted in volunteer troops from Iowa, Kansas and Ohio being sent to patrol the area. The first detachment to arrive at Guinard's Bridge and the telegraph station was Company D of the Sixth Ohio Volunteer Cavalry, commanded by Lieutenant Colonel William Collins. The troops quickly built their own quarters and fortifications, and the post was known as Platte Bridge Station, after the telegraph station of the same name.[46]

The destruction of telegraph lines soon spread from the Shoshoni to other tribes, including the Sioux, Cheyenne and Arapaho. This, in turn, kept the soldiers quite busy during the summer of 1862 repairing lines. Charles Whitehead, a former member of Companies E and L of the Eleventh Ohio Volunteer Cavalry, described the Native Americans' method of attack in great detail. He wrote that the Native Americans would toss a strong rope over the frail telegraph wire, hook it and then take off on their ponies at a full gallop. They would then take the torn section of wire, coil it up and hide it somewhere nearby. After the wire was hidden, they would start a fire of sagebrush or greasewood at the base of the pole until it burned through and fell. Soldiers often witnessed this from their outposts but did not dare venture out to repair the lines until they had the cover of darkness.[47]

The act of repairing the telegraph lines was carried out in the utmost secrecy and silence. Whitehead also described this process fairly well in a newspaper interview. He wrote that the horses' hooves were sometimes muffled with padding in order to minimize noise. The soldiers often rode without saddles so that the horses would be lighter and able to run faster in case of an ambush. If they were ambushed, they had instructions to split up and make their way back to camp as quietly as possible in order to avoid detection. To repair the line, the soldiers would reuse the burned telegraph pole by inserting it into a freshly dug hole and stringing the wire along a new nail on the side of the pole. The soldiers also padded their hammers so as not to make additional noise pounding nails into the pole. Often, the thin fragile wire wrapped in silk was strewn across the tops of sagebrush and weeds and would be broken by stray animals.

Repairing telegraph lines was dangerous work, and men had to be on the lookout for Native American attacks while away from the safety of the fort. *Library of Congress.*

The men were not allowed to talk during the entire operation and only whispered when absolutely necessary.[18]

Hostility with the tribes continued as they began attacking mail carriers and stations. Three Crossings Station was raided and burned to the ground. The decision was made to change the overland mail route in the hopes to

This photo, taken around 1870, depicts the remnants of Three Crossings Station. *Wyoming State Archives, Department of State Parks and Cultural Resources.*

avoid future incidents like the one at Three Crossings Station. In moving the mail route farther south, Guinard's Bridge was no longer on the route, which affected his revenue. However, many westward travelers continued to use his bridge crossing, necessitating the presence of a military detachment.[49]

By October 1862, the detachment of twenty-eight men at Platte Bridge under Captain Peter Van Winkle had settled in for the winter. The construction of personnel quarters and stables for thirty-five horses and six mules had been completed, and the men had sufficient rations to last until April. Just one short month later, Van Winkle's garrison had nearly doubled to include sixty-nine men and sixty-two horses.[50]

The detachment at Platte Bridge Station passed the year of 1863 fairly quietly. Peace treaties with the Ute and Shoshoni tribes removed them as threats to the post. Hostile tribes in the area included the Sioux, Northern Cheyenne and Arapaho. The only major skirmish of note in the area during this year occurred at Sweetwater Station. On April 3, the station was

This drawing by bugler Moellman in 1863 depicts Platte Bridge Station and Guinard's Bridge. *Wyoming State Archives, Department of State Parks and Cultural Resources.*

attacked, and Private Ira Grossman of Company B, Eleventh Ohio, was mortally wounded during the engagement.[51]

Lieutenant Colonel William Collins saw an opportunity to recruit more men into the Ohio cavalry during the summer of 1863 given the relative calm in the Rocky Mountain region. A broadside recruiting poster in Ohio advertised a "service full of novelty and adventure" and touted the health benefits of the high altitude of the territory by claiming that it is "especially beneficial to those having a tendency to pulmonary complaints and the effect upon all, is to invigorate the constitution and prolong life."[52]

By July, Collins had succeeded in organizing a Second Independent Battalion of Ohio Volunteer Cavalry. The new Companies E, F, G and H were consolidated to form the Eleventh Ohio Volunteer Cavalry. Still, Collins was fifty men short of the required number for his new regiment. He chose to offer the chance of service to Ohio's Confederate prisoners of war in order to fill the void. Many of those prisoners chose to enlist and were known as "Galvanized Yankees."[53]

Company G of the Eleventh Ohio, under the command of First Lieutenant Henry Clay Bretney, patrolled a distance of approximately 150 miles along the Oregon Trail from Platte Bridge to South Pass Station. The company consisted of 105 men, 92 of whom were under the age of twenty-three. Outposts along this stretch were manned by between 4 and 10 men along with a telegraph operator. Company G's main prerogative was to ensure that the telegraph system remained operational and to repair any broken lines.[54]

First Lieutenant Bretney was well liked by his men, spoke fluent French and German and played a good game of poker. James Patton (an enlisted man) felt that he was always concerned with the welfare of his men and generally appreciated more by the privates of the regiment than the officers.[55]

Bretney's second in command was Second Lieutenant Caspar W. Collins, the son of Lieutenant Colonel William O. Collins, in command of the

Lieutenant Henry Clay Bretney, Eleventh Ohio Cavalry. *Fort Caspar Museum.*

Eleventh Ohio. From a young age, Caspar had seemingly always wanted to join the military, despite his parents' protests. Eventually, his persistence got the better of his parents, and they agreed to let seventeen-year-old Caspar accompany his father as a civilian on his duties throughout the West. This was Caspar's first experience living outside Hillsboro, Ohio, for any length of time. Originally not an official member of the battalion, Caspar served as a "clerk, engineer and draughtsman without compensation until June 1863 when he entered the service."[56] Caspar was mustered in as a second lieutenant a couple months shy of his nineteenth birthday in July 1863.[57]

Living in Wyoming often took some getting used to for the troops from Ohio. Winters were bitterly cold, and the posts were extremely isolated from any sort of town or civilization. The winter of 1863–64 was especially brutal on the garrison. "At Fort Laramie, soldiers of the 11th Ohio found that on the nights of January 3, 4, and 5, the mercury froze for four hours, fifteen hours, and twelve hours respectively."[58] "One soldier reported that, 'We had a wood pile only a hundred yards or so from the Barracks and men would freeze their hands, feet and ears just going over there and chopping wood a little while, not very much while, they would take three or four strokes when they would have to run back to camp."[59] Conditions were even worse traveling between posts. A quartermaster's report of supplies illustrates the poor supplies available to both the men and their horses, writing, "Each man had only one wool blanket, one gum blanket and an overcoat. It snowed and there was no wood for a fire but scant sagebrush, which was a stubborn proposition if one tried to make it burn. The horses were in woeful condition, having had no corn for a month."[60]

Ben Arnold, whose job in 1863 was to care for the horses at Platte Bridge Station, described the isolation of the post in his journals. The time seemed to drag on forever, and he wrote, "We lost track of the days, the weeks, even the months. I never knew when Christmas or New Year's passed by. We were completely shut off from the outside."[61]

By March 1864, Lieutenant Bretney was in command of Platte Bridge Station and would remain there for a little over a year. During this time, an increase in traffic along the Bozeman and Bridger Trails began to aggravate the relationships with local Native American tribes.

That summer, some Miniconjou began attacking travelers along the Oregon Trail. To combat this new threat, the Eleventh Ohio gained additional troops in order to create the new companies of I, K and L. In early July 1864, the Larimer wagon train was attacked, four men were killed and a woman by the name of Fanny Kelley was abducted. Lieutenant

Construction of Platte Bridge Station, Camp Dodge and Escalation of Violence

John Brown was dispatched from Platte Bridge Station on July 13 with two companies of men to intercept the raiders and rescue Mrs. Kelley. Lieutenant Brown and his men arrived six days later at Cheyenne Fork and made camp. Unfortunately, they arrived too late to rescue Mrs. Kelley or find the attackers. The next morning, Lieutenant Brown and thirteen of his men were ambushed at a nearby spring by Sioux warriors. Wounded in the neck by an arrow, Brown was left behind by his men as they fled the attack. The next day, Brown was found still alive by a search party, but he succumbed to his wounds the following day.[62]

Relations between the military and the Sioux further soured that same month when Lieutenant Bretney held a peace conference with Brule Sioux chief Old Grass. The conference was intended to solidify the peaceful relationship already enjoyed between them, but things went awry when a soldier accidentally discharged his weapon during the event. No one was injured, but the incident angered Old Grass to the point that he and his band left the conference. Enraged, Old Grass is reported to have told Bretney that he would someday have his scalp. From this point on, Old Grass began to advocate for violence and war against the pioneers and military.[63]

These events set in motion the eventual abandonment of John Richard's trading post and bridge crossing. In August 1864, Old Grass was wounded in the thigh in a skirmish, and another chief, Red Shell, and two of his family members were killed. Lieutenant Bretney hoped that by taking Sioux hostages he would force Old Grass and his followers to surrender. Because Richard was married to a Sioux woman, his family (seven persons), along with Stone Belly and his family (six persons), Milk and family (five persons) and Rocky Bear and family (five persons), were rounded up and sent to Fort Laramie. Richard was released soon after, but the event seemed to have been the final straw for him and his family. By the spring of 1865, Richard had relocated to an area about twenty miles west of the city of Laramie and set up a new trading post there. He left his store and bridge crossing with others to manage and completely left the area.[64]

A few months later, a momentous event occurred on the plains that would resonate throughout the area, and especially at Platte Bridge. On November 29, 1864, Colonel John Chivington and his command descended on a band of Southern Cheyenne in southeastern Colorado. The Cheyenne were caught unaware, and roughly two hundred were dead when the fighting ended. The Colorado troops brought back scalps and severed genitals of the deceased Cheyenne to Denver, where they were met with great applause. Naturally, the U.S. government disapproved of such a crime, but no charges were pressed against Chivington, as he was no longer in the military.[65]

The Sand Creek Massacre, as it came to be known, did little more than enrage the tribes throughout the plains and Rocky Mountain region. It provided them with a single unifying event to rally their tribes and declare open war against the whites. It forged an alliance of the Sioux, Cheyenne and Arapaho tribes throughout the region. "Outrage at the massacre was so great that the tribes determined to begin their offensive during the winter months, a very unusual tactic in Indian warfare up to that point."[66]

Recalling this period forty years later, one member of Company G (Eleventh Ohio) wrote, "The Indians at that time were on the war-path and worse than at any time in their history, either before or since. It was almost a daily occurrence for some of our company to have a brush with them."[67]

Beginning in early 1865, the Plains Indians began a series of retaliatory strikes against U.S. military outposts and civilians. In January and February, the town of Julesburg was sacked by bands of Cheyenne, Sioux and Arapaho, reducing it to ruins.[68] Colonel William Collins of the Eleventh Ohio Volunteer Cavalry believed that the Cheyenne and Sioux had headed toward the Powder River, where he thought they would continue to harass military personnel and civilians until dealt with. Colonel Collins wrote, "They are well armed and mounted [and] have many rifled muskets and plenty of ammunition including Minnie cartridges with ounce balls, [and] are full of venom bent on revenge for the loss of their people south. The posts on the Platte especially Deer Creek and Platte Bridge will be in immediate danger."[69] Colonel Collins could not have been more right with his prediction, the results of which would affect him very personally.

During the spring of 1865, Platte Bridge Station underwent a bit of an expansion and remodel as new buildings were added and existing structures were improved. The station included a long twelve- by thirty-two-foot building containing a telegraph office, telegraph operator's bedroom, kitchen/storeroom and a lean-to to store telegraph supplies.[70] Improvements continued into the summer, when the post consisted of the original log buildings surrounded by a log stockade approximately twenty feet tall that served as protection for the men and a corral for the horses. William Y. Drew, who lived at Platte Bridge Station during the summer of 1865, described it simply as "a stockade inside of which were accommodations for a garrison of about one hundred men."[71] When the improvements were finally completed, the post consisted of a permanent post made up of two stores, each one hundred feet square; a blacksmith shop with an adjoining

Reconstructed telegraph room at Fort Caspar Museum. *Author's collection.*

corral built of pine logs; a stable; a corral forty-five by forty-eight feet; two officers' rooms; a laundry; a private room; a commissary; two squad rooms; a kitchen; a storeroom; a telegraph office; and a telegraph wareroom.[72]

By early 1865, Colonel Collins had given his young son (not yet twenty years of age) command of the four small telegraph outposts north of Platte Bridge Station. According to Private Hervey Johnson of the Eleventh Ohio, the young lieutenant was "a smart scholar but a perfect boy, and entirely incapable of holding the position of Lieutenant."[73]

Hostilities with the tribes continued to result in minor skirmishes throughout the winter and early spring of 1865. On February 13, Company G of the Eleventh Ohio engaged horse-stealing warriors near La Prele Creek. Captain Levi M. Rinehart, the commander, was shot through the heart and lungs in a pre-dawn charge against the campsite. Due to Captain Rinehart's death, Lieutenant Bretney assumed command of Company G.[74]

In another instance, Privates William (Billie) T. Kame and Philip W. Rhodes, also of Company G, Eleventh Ohio, were attacked near Poison Creek on their way to Sweetwater Station to deliver supplies. Nearly halfway to their destination, the two men were approached by four Arapaho claiming to be friendly, but when they were close to the wagon, they opened fire, killing Rhodes instantly. Kame grabbed his Spencer carbine and held off his assailants through the afternoon until dark. Surviving with only a bullet hole through his shirt, he saddled the wagon's horse and rode to Sweetwater Station, arriving around midnight. Lieutenant Caspar Collins commanded a detachment of the company at Sweetwater Station and took four men to return to the scene of the ambush in order to pursue the attackers, but to no avail. Collins informed Lieutenant Bretney at Platte Bridge of the skirmish via telegraph, and Bretney left with a detachment to retrieve the slain Private Rhodes's body. The snowy weather was terrible, and "Pvt. C.B. Cook later wrote that the march was 'the worst thing I ever was in,' and remembered that 'the only way we could keep from being lost was by keeping sight of the man and horse ahead of us.'"[75] Bretney and his detachment eventually found Rhodes's body, and it was returned to the fort.[76]

The almost continuous skirmishes took a toll on the military generals and department heads. By the spring of 1865, the Civil War was winding down, and the War Department began to shift its focus out west and was willing to commit more resources to the frontier. It faced a problem with manpower, however, as the units serving in the West were volunteer—meaning that once their three-year enlistments were up, they were free to go. Most of these men joined hoping to fight the Confederacy in 1862 but were sent west instead. Entire companies of troops were being mustered out, and it was clear that the western territories would need reinforcements. Four companies of the Eleventh Ohio (A, B, C and D) were mustered out in Omaha, Nebraska, on April 1, 1865. The Eleventh Kansas, commanded by Colonel Thomas Moonlight, was ordered to fill that gap. On April 9, the regiment arrived at Fort Laramie to begin its duty protecting the trails and telegraph lines heading west.[77]

Colonel Moonlight was a character with a somewhat dubious reputation. Moonlight immigrated to the United States from Scotland at the age of thirteen and served as an enlisted man during the Seminole War. He left the service in 1859 in order to farm in Kansas but returned to the military at the beginning of the Civil War. In September 1862, he was appointed lieutenant colonel of the Eleventh Kansas Infantry, which was later redesignated the Eleventh Kansas Cavalry. Personally, he had the reputation "of a man of action who liked his liquor."[78] The regiment's journey to Fort Laramie was fraught with danger due to blizzards and subzero temperatures. Men suffered from frostbite and would become lost in heavy snowdrifts, requiring search parties to locate them. The regiment had no wood for fires at night and was forced to camp in the snow.[79] Moonlight was angered by the roughly six-week ride from Fort Riley to Fort Laramie and wrote, "This, I presume, was a reward of merit for their gallantry

Thomas Moonlight, Eleventh Kansas Cavalry. *Library of Congress.*

and devotion during the border campaign. I look upon it as the greatest outrage that was perpetuated on any regiment."[80]

The men of the Eleventh Kansas were no stranger to action. Prior to their assignment in present-day Wyoming, they had fought hard against Confederate general Sterling Price and tangled with Quantrill's raiders. They had participated in several battles, including the Second Battle of Lexington and the Battle of Westport, and had routed Confederate forces in Indiana and throughout the Midwest.[81]

Lieutenant Colonel Preston B. Plumb, Eleventh Kansas Cavalry. *Kansas State Historical Society.*

Lieutenant Colonel Preston Plumb had participated in all of the above engagements and was an officer who held the utmost respect from his men. Colonel William Denison of the Eleventh Kansas was also fond of Plumb and had met him when the regiment first formed in 1862. He described Plumb as full of "energy, good sense, practical ideas, hopefulness and enthusiasm."[82] Denison also described the unofficial motto of the Eleventh Kansas as "On with the dance!" a quotation from Lord Byron's "The Eve of Waterloo" and one of Plumb's favorites.[83]

In February 1865, the Eleventh Kansas began moving from Fort Riley to Fort Kearney. It moved through a rainstorm that quickly became one of the worst blizzards in the area. Many of the wagons became stuck in the mud, and the soldiers were forced to sit out the storm. The next morning, the storm had stopped, and Colonel Plumb "ordered the bugler to call retreat but the bugle being full of ice failed to work."[84] The next day, the men were forced to build a bridge using forty-foot-long logs, brush, grass and dirt in order to cross a dangerous creek. According to Thomas Barber, Company C, Eleventh Kansas, "Col. P.B. [Preston Plumb] threw more dirt than any of us and proved himself a real bridge builder."[85]

Later that year, the Eleventh Kansas was ordered to protect the road between Fort Laramie and Platte Bridge Station. Detachments were posted at Horseshoe Creek, La Bonte, Deer Creek and Sweetwater Station. Lieutenant Colonel Preston Plumb chose a site between five and seven miles from Platte Bridge Station to serve as regimental headquarters, called Camp Dodge.

Camp Dodge and its commander have both seemingly been lost to history in favor of the more well-known Platte Bridge Station. Today, the location of Camp Dodge remains unknown, but William Connelley's biography of

Preston Plumb provides the best clues. He describes it as about "seven miles from Platte Bridge, near the foothills of the Laramie range, where wood and water were at hand."[86] The best guess for the camp's location is that it was near where the east and west forks of Garden Creek join, on the property of the former Carpenter Ranch.[87] He also writes that Platte Bridge Station was in plain view of the camp and a twenty-one-minute horse ride at full gallop.[88] Plumb personally selected the camp's location and named it in honor of General Grenville Dodge, who was the commander of the Department of the Missouri. He and his troops arrived there in mid- to late April with only enough rations for twenty days, which were expected to last throughout the summer. In addition, the ammunition for the carbines used by the Eleventh Kansas had not arrived from Fort Leavenworth.[89] Despite these conditions, Colonel Plumb proved to be an excellent commander and played an important role in the events of the summer of 1865.

Preston Bierce Plumb was born on October 12, 1837, in Berkshire, Ohio, the eldest child of working-class parents David and Hannah Maria (Bierce) Plumb. Young Preston's life was full of learning and adventure. He possessed a daring and studious spirit and excelled in his school classes and other endeavors. At the age of ten, he went with some friends to the woods for the Fourth of July. In the wood was a large barn holding two chained pet bears and some swings for children. While he was pushing some of the other children on the swings, he slipped and fell right into the bears. One of the bears grabbed him and proceeded to maul him. Luckily, the other bear took the opportunity to start fighting with the bear holding him, and Plumb was able to roll away to safety. His wounds were so severe that he was not expected to survive. To his dying day, he carried tooth and claw scars from this incident.[90]

His father had hoped that Plumb would continue in the family wagon-making business, but with the encouragement of his mother, he had other plans. At age eleven, he attended Kenyon College, a preparatory school, and learned the trade of printing. While there, he worked in the printing industry to pay for his tuition. After three years, he returned to Marysville, where he worked for the local paper, the *Tribune*, and afterward purchased and edited the *Xenia News*.[91]

Portrait of Preston Plumb while serving as a U.S. senator from Kansas.
Library of Congress.

He moved to Lawrence, Kansas, in 1856 to support the "Free-State" movement. He had met John Brown and became enamored in his cause. During that time, he smuggled weapons and supplies from Ohio into Kansas to support Brown. He was one of the founders of Emporia, Kansas, where he established the *Kansas News* in 1857. While only twenty years old, he was secretary of the Free-State convention in 1857 and a member of the Leavenworth constitutional convention in 1859. This was an especially important session since, as the name implies, the constitution of the state of Kansas was formalized that year. By the age of twenty-two, Plumb had not only bought a newspaper, helped found the city of Emporia and smuggled weapons for John Brown, but he had also participated in the legislative session that finalized the constitution of the state of Kansas.

Plumb studied law and was admitted to the bar in 1861. He was elected to the Kansas House of Representatives in 1862 and was a reporter for the Kansas Supreme Court. At this time, he enlisted in the Eleventh Kansas Cavalry (originally an infantry regiment) and began his military service.

Following the war, Plumb was mostly interested in the cattle business and had planned on giving up politics. His friend Stotler encouraged Plumb to run as a candidate for the state legislature. Plumb was busy with his brother George in the cattle business and did not reply to Stotler's requests, hoping that his friend would simply drop the issue. Undeterred, Stotler put Plumb's name in the race, and the opposing candidate began to circulate reports that Plumb was no longer involved in the city of Emporia and that he did not care about Emporia at all. As soon as Plumb heard this, he immediately left his ranch and, along with his brother, on the morning of the election made his presence known at the ballot locations. The majority of the voters were men who had served in the Eleventh Kansas, and Plumb was elected in a landslide margin of nearly two to one.[92] He served in the state House of Representatives in 1867 and 1868 and served as Speaker in the latter year. During that session, he oversaw major rebuilding and construction in the state of Kansas. The legislature dealt with damages incurred in the Civil War, forty-three county boundary changes and many other miscellaneous issues.[93]

During this time, Plumb met Caroline Southwick, the daughter of staunch abolitionist Abijah Southwick. His home was a principal stop along the Underground Railroad in Massachusetts. Plumb married Southwick on March 8, 1867, and they had six children.[94]

In 1867, Plumb also became a partner in the Ruggles and Plumb law firm in Emporia. The firm was one of the most successful in Kansas, and Plumb was regarded as a fine lawyer. He would often ride on horseback across the state and into neighboring states to meet with clients and try cases. Through this business, Plumb became acquainted with nearly every well-to-do family in Kansas. He was also prosecuting attorney of Lyon County.[95]

Plumb secured a charter from Washington, D.C., for the Emporia National Bank in June 1872. Once the charter was secured, Plumb became president of the bank and scaled back from his practice of law. The financial crisis of 1873 nearly destroyed the bank, but through Plumb's resourcefulness, it was saved. None of his clients was forced into bankruptcy; he saved many from that fate. Numerous accounts show that, unlike many banks, Plumb was willing to lend money to those in need and supported a number of small businesses through financial difficulties.[96]

One of Plumb's neighbors described an instance of Plumb's generosity. His neighbor had taken out a homestead, but his work required him to be away from it for long periods of time. His friends worried that his claim would be jumped in his absence and urged him to buy the land. The land cost $250, but he only had $50 to his name. He tried to get a loan from the bank, but since he could offer no security, he was denied. He wrote, "I went back to work and watched for Colonel Plumb to come by on his way to dinner and when he passed I followed him around the corner and explained my needs. 'Come into the bank when I get back,' said Plumb. I did so, and he told the cashier to let me have the money. That money saved my home."[97]

In 1877, Preston Plumb was elected as a Republican to the U.S. Senate; he was reelected in 1883 and 1888 and served from March 4, 1877, until his death in 1891. While in the Senate, he was on the Military Affairs Committee, Mines and Mining Committee and chairman of the Committee on Public Lands (Forty-seventh through Fifty-second Congresses).

Plumb suffered from severe headaches and health issues toward the end of his life. Some believed that these problems were brought on by overwork, as he worked tirelessly on the issues that he cared about. On December 20, 1891, Preston Plumb passed away at his home in Washington, D.C. A memorial attended by many members of the Senate and the Supreme Court, as well as the vice president and president of the United States, was held in a small room in the Capitol Building. Many of his colleagues in Washington remembered him fondly and were deeply shocked and saddened by his death.[98]

His body was later moved to Kansas for a funeral and burial in Maplewood Cemetery in Emporia. When the body arrived by train in Topeka, it was met by members of the Grand Army of the Republic, Knights Templar and Eleventh Kansas Cavalry. In addition, approximately fifteen thousand mourners arrived at the train station to escort his body to his Emporia home. The casket was draped with the original battle standard of the Eleventh Kansas Cavalry—still tattered and war torn—a silent witness to Plumb's military legacy. Members of the Eleventh Kansas Cavalry stood guard day and night both inside and outside the house until the body was escorted to the church for the funeral service. He was buried in Maplewood Cemetery in Emporia.[99]

Preston Plumb's legacy is a long and important one. Most people can only hope to achieve a fraction of the success that he attained during his lifetime—from owning and operating his own newspaper, serving in the Kansas legislature, becoming a successful attorney, serving the U.S. Army as a renowned cavalry officer and becoming president of a bank to ending his illustrious career as a popular U.S. senator. Perhaps the most striking aspect of Preston Plumb's character is the fact that he was able to accomplish all of the above without losing his humanity and connection with the common people. He retained a strong sense of humility throughout his life and was known both for his strength of character as well as his generosity.

In April 1865, Moonlight was appointed commander of the north subdistrict of the Great Plains and had his headquarters in Fort Laramie. Lieutenant Colonel Plumb served as his second in command at Camp Dodge. Content with his new position, Colonel Moonlight set out on an offensive raid throughout his district against the Native Americans. On May 3, he organized an expedition of five hundred cavalry of the Eleventh Kansas, Eleventh Ohio and Seventh Iowa to the Wind River to attempt to disperse a camp of Cheyenne rumored to be in the valley of that river. Moonlight believed that defeating and dispersing the roughly three hundred lodges would give peace to the overland trails.[100] Moonlight's expedition in cold and snowy weather included Lieutenant Colonel Plumb, Major Martin Anderson, Major Adams and Lieutenant Bretney and twenty men of Company G, Eleventh Ohio, from Platte Bridge Station. Moonlight's poor leadership spurred a rivalry between the Eleventh Kansas and the Eleventh Ohio that was further cemented on his expedition. According to a member of Company K of the Eleventh Ohio, one incident destroyed that relationship even further. It seems that Moonlight mistook a herd of antelope for a war party of Native Americans and sent Bretney's detachment to investigate rather than a detachment of the Eleventh Kansas.[101] Despite Moonlight's belief that a large number of Cheyenne were camping in the area, his scouts, and even famed mountain man Jim Bridger (who accompanied the expedition), could find no sign of them or their camp. Conditions on the expedition were also extremely difficult. Water was in short supply, and many of the men threatened mutiny against Moonlight, saying, "Moonlight, we are not going to follow you; there is too much damn moonlight here," referencing the bright moon and Moonlight's poor leadership. Frustrated and exhausted, Moonlight unofficially relinquished command to Plumb. Plumb immediately led the party east toward the mountains and water. The thirsty horses and men at once plunged into the spring snow and fresh stream and camped for forty-eight hours. Prior to finding water, Major Anderson had drank from an alkali stream and burned his mouth severely. Plumb had a can of tomatoes and warmed up the can on a campfire, thinking that the tomatoes would soothe Anderson's burned mouth. Plumb became sidetracked talking to another soldier and forgot about the hot tomato can on the fire. Just as he remembered and went to retrieve it, it exploded, sending tomato bits flying into the cottonwood tree above the campfire. Undeterred, Plumb scooped up as many of the tomato bits as he could find and served them on crackers to the sick troops.[102]

By the end of the month, the entire party had returned to its station never having fired a shot. After his return to Fort Laramie, Moonlight was still convinced that a large party of Native Americans was on the prowl ready to attack. He wrote in his report of the expedition that they had simply arrived too late and reiterated his desire to wage a sizeable campaign and even establish a new fort:

> *Striking Powder River about one hundred miles north of where I was, that is north of here and west where a large and strong fort should be built… The Cheyenne and Sioux who are with them will number about (4000) four thousand fighting men. No time to be lost in making campaign but horses are in poor condition, having had no corn for a month.*[103]

Moonlight's "shoot first and ask questions later" strategy for dealing with Native American tribes would soon prove to incite even more hostilities in his district. Only a few days after having written the report of his failed Wind River expedition, Colonel Moonlight made another egregious command error. While he was still on his expedition, on May 15 scouts from Fort Laramie discovered a small band of Sioux about ten miles from the fort. Among the Sioux were Mrs. Lucinda Ewbanks and her small daughter who had been kidnapped by the Cheyenne in Nebraska about nine months earlier. The scouts brought in Two Face's Oglalas, who had been holding

Mrs. Ewbanks, as well as Black Foot and a few from his band, for a total of six men in confinement.[104]

Mrs. Ewbanks was in extremely poor health and nearly naked when she was discovered. According to Lieutenant Henry Palmer, "Her back, as shown to General Connor and myself, was a mass of raw sores from her neck to her waist, where she had been whipped and beaten by Two Faces' squaws. The sores had not been permitted to heal and were a sight most sickening to behold. The poor woman was crushed in spirit and almost a maniac."[105] Supposedly, Two Face had purchased Mrs. Ewbanks from the Cheyenne as a gesture of friendliness, but she claimed that she had been horribly mistreated at the hands of the Sioux. She was given the money that Two Face and Black Foot and their Oglalas had on them, which amounted to $270. The Oglalas also had in their possession six U.S. mules, three U.S. horses and five likely stolen unbranded mules.[106]

On May 25, Moonlight ordered that Two Face and Black Foot were to be executed the next day. He intended for the hangings to be "an example to all Indians of like character and in retaliation for the many wrongs and outrages they have committed on the white race."[107] Despite warnings from local traders that the hangings would trigger even more retaliation, Moonlight persisted. "Moonlight noted that, 'Both of the chiefs openly boasted that they had killed white men and that they would do it again if let loose.' Consequently, in his words, he concluded 'to tie them by the neck with trace chains, suspended from a beam of wood, and leave them there without any foothold.'"[108] True to his word, Moonlight left the decaying corpses of Two Face and Black Foot dangling at the fort for months in public view.[109]

By the next day, it was clear that Moonlight's strategy of making an example of Two Face and Black Foot had failed. Approximately 150 Native Americans attacked and burned the telegraph station of Rocky Ridge. The station was manned by five men of Company G, Eleventh Ohio, who made a hasty escape underground. Luckily for the soldiers, they had a nearby earth cellar to hide in while the fire spread to their ammunition stores. The resulting explosions managed to scare off the attackers, and all five men survived. Unfortunately, the two dogs living with the Eleventh Ohio men perished in their quarters. Private Chavil St. Clair managed to salvage a telegraph key and some wire and was able to communicate with Fort Bridger about the attack once it was safe. The men eventually escaped to South Pass.[110]

Colonel Moonlight's response to this incident also served to fuel resentment between the Eleventh Ohio and the Eleventh Kansas. St. Clair complained that due to the fact that he and the rest of his detachment were separated from the ammunition, they were unable to retaliate successfully against their attackers. Colonel Moonlight called this simply a "convenient excuse" and expressed his anger to the acting assistant adjutant general in a letter, writing, "Every officer who has had stock taken from him by Indians unless in extreme cases should be dismissed from the service."[111] Moonlight was quick to point out that his regiment, the Eleventh Kansas, had not lost any stock and had managed to kill several warriors. This left the obvious conclusion that he was referring to the only other regiment on this route—the Eleventh Ohio.[112]

Raids continued in the next week all along the route. Elkhorn Station was attacked, horses and mules were stolen from Sweetwater Station, Pole Creek was attacked and the entire army herd was stolen from the Laramie Peak sawmill. In response, security was increased at Platte Bridge Station, and a noncommissioned officer was dispatched to the former Platte River crossing at Richard's Bridge as a lookout. Despite these increases in security, a wagon train was attacked twice while en route from Platte Bridge to Fort Laramie, and three hundred warriors attacked Three Crossings Station. The situation had clearly devolved to the point where it was no longer safe for travelers to pass along these routes. All emigrant travel was halted near Julesburg, Colorado, and only those who were affiliated with the government were allowed to pass. Settlers and commercial traffic were directed to use the Overland Mail Road instead.[113]

Lieutenant Colonel Plumb took charge of the situation and dispersed his men throughout the area in order to repair the telegraph line and rebuild the station at Rocky Ridge after the horrific attack a few days prior. Plumb reported the event to Fort Laramie and wrote that Lieutenant Caspar Collins went from Three Crossings Station to Rocky Ridge to investigate and look for survivors, but he only got close enough to see the station burning and did not consider it prudent to venture any closer. It took a few days before the survivors were discovered and rescued. Had Lieutenant Collins ridden farther toward the burned station, he would have likely seen the survivors and been able to rescue them much sooner. The attacks continued, and just a few days later, forty warriors stampeded the horses and mules at Sweetwater Station. One Native American was killed in that attack.[114]

On June 3, 1865, the attacks reached Platte Bridge Station. At approximately 3:00 p.m., ten warriors rode up to the riverbank opposite Platte Bridge Station and opened fire. The troops forced the warriors to retreat and returned fire with carbines and the mountain howitzer. Fearing a major attack, First Sergeant S.B. White sent a corporal and ten men of

Construction of Platte Bridge Station, Camp Dodge and Escalation of Violence

Illustration of Sweetwater Station. *Wyoming State Archives, Department of State Parks and Cultural Resources.*

Company G, Eleventh Ohio, in pursuit with instructions to keep track of the warriors' movements until Lieutenant Colonel Plumb and reinforcements at Camp Dodge could be informed of the attack.[115] Upon receiving the messenger, Plumb set out at once for the post and ordered thirty of his men to follow him. At the bridge, he picked up ten more men and pursued the attackers for approximately five miles before finally coming within firing range. The troops managed to kill a horse and wound two warriors, but in the hot pursuit, Plumb had become separated from half of his detachment. The warriors used this to their advantage and turned and charged at Plumb and the men whose horses had been able to keep up the hard pursuit. Plumb fired a volley at the advancing warriors to allow him and his men the chance to escape. As they turned and fled, sixty previously obscured warriors emerged and chased them down Dry Creek (slightly to the left of Plumb's position), trying to cut them off from the fort. At the last moment, the men from Camp Dodge who had been separated from Plumb caught up with them, and the warriors called off their attack. Seven soldiers continued on to pursue the fleeing warriors but were led into an ambush resulting in the deaths of two of the men: Private Bonwell of the Eleventh Kansas and Private Stahlnecker of the Eleventh Ohio.[116]

According to Plumb's description of the battle location, it was somewhere near the current Natrona County International Airport,

The guidon of the Eleventh Kansas Cavalry. *Kansas State Historical Society.*

which is about ten miles from the likely location of Camp Dodge near Garden Creek by Casper Mountain.[117]

Three days after the attack on June 3, Louis Guinard (proprietor of the bridge crossing at Platte Bridge Station) drowned. Guinard's nephew described the family version of events in 1911: "My uncle and my father went out on the bridge one night to have a talk and my uncle 'fell' over into the water and was drowned. My father then took charge of the store at the trading post nearby the fort, which was owned by my uncle, and he also took all of his other property."[118] Guinard's body was never found, but several months later, his leg and foot surfaced inside one of his boots. The remains were given to his widow, "who hung the boot on the wall and mourned over it in Indian fashion."[119]

Camp Dodge was abandoned by the Eleventh Kansas Cavalry shortly after this incident in mid-June. Colonel Plumb received orders to go to Fort Halleck and to bring Companies A, B, F, L and M with him. He established regimental headquarters at La Bonte station (near present-day Douglas, Wyoming) at the end of June. Plumb's new orders did not include direct management of Platte Bridge Station, so he never returned to that post.[120]

During this same time, Colonel Moonlight led another failed attempt to chase down attacking Sioux. Gathering a force of California and Ohio Cavalry in addition to his own Kansas Cavalry, he set out from Fort Laramie with nearly 250 men. However, his "chase" averaged a speed of two and a half miles per hour, and some officers complained that in addition to the gruelingly slow pace, Moonlight was drunk a majority of the time. The situation became even worse when a band of 200 Sioux surprised Moonlight and his camp and succeeded in stampeding half of the group's horses. Following this, they were forced to return to Fort Laramie, with half of the men making the journey on foot. General Connor became enraged upon learning of this debacle and immediately relieved Moonlight of command and moved his headquarters to Fort Laramie to provide greater oversight of the North Subdistrict of the West. Colonel Moonlight was mustered out of the service shortly after being relieved of command.[121]

Things were quickly heating up near Platte Bridge Station and the smaller surrounding telegraph outposts. Deer Creek Station was attacked on June 15, and Private Silas Henshaw of Company A, Eleventh Kansas, was killed while he was out gathering wood. Five days later, somewhere between forty and seventy-five Shoshoni attacked the eight men of Company G, Eleventh Ohio, posted at Sweetwater Station. The telegraph operator and three Arapaho were killed during the skirmish. Edgar Gwynn, the telegraph operator, was horribly mutilated during the attack: "They scalped all the hair of his head, and cut off his hands at the wrists, took the sinews out of arms, took out his heart and liver, ran a lance into him and stuck him up on a pole."[122]

The attacks continued into July and soon focused on Platte Bridge Station. On July 2, Captain Greer of the Eleventh Kansas and 10 men chased a group of Sioux who had cut telegraph wires and fired shots at the post. Similar to the fight that occurred on June 3, Captain Greer and his men pursued the small band of Sioux to the site of the old Post at Platte Bridge and Richard's crossing but soon found themselves in the face of an ambush of a considerably larger force of Sioux. The soldiers were forced to make a hasty retreat back to Platte Bridge Station while skirmishing with warriors along the way. Only one soldier was wounded: Sergeant John Holding, who received a gunshot wound to his lower ear.[123] The same day as this attack, Major Anderson ordered an increase in men at Platte Bridge Station. Three more companies of the Eleventh Kansas were sent to the post, bringing the total garrison to around 120 men.[124]

Although Lieutenant Bretney is hailed as a hero for his actions at the Battle of Platte Bridge (which will be discussed later), he also had quite the temper. As mentioned previously, tensions were high between the Eleventh Kansas and Eleventh Ohio, largely due to the failed leadership of Colonel Moonlight of the Eleventh Kansas.

On July 12, Lieutenant Bretney, along with a detachment from Company G of the Eleventh Ohio, arrived at Platte Bridge Station. Upon his arrival at the post, he was upset to see a number of civilian settlers camping along the river near the fort. For unknown reasons, he did not want them there and gave a written order to his men of Company G that he wanted them moved. Captain Greer of the Eleventh Kansas was the ranking officer in command of the post and had already given the settlers permission to camp one mile or farther from the fort. Lieutenant Bretney became irate and attempted to take command of the post. Captain Greer informed him that he had given permission to the emigrants to camp there and that it did not concern Lieutenant Bretney. Bretney responded by insulting Greer and yelling that he did not care who was in command, he was going to make those people leave. At this point, Bretney and a number of his men of Company G were quite drunk and left the fort, heading toward the emigrant camp. Once there, they fired several shots into the camp, narrowly missing two persons and a young child. Another Eleventh Ohio soldier fired at the settlers from the bridge, narrowly missing more people. Bretney stormed into the telegraph office twice, threatening to shoot the telegraph operator. The telegraph operator, Kelly, ran out of the office and was granted permission to sleep with Captain Greer and Sergeant Pennock, as he was fearful for his life. Bretney's actions created a dangerous situation at the fort, and it was very lucky that no one was seriously hurt. Sergeant Pennock wrote in his diary that "the emegrants [*sic*] asked protection of Capt. Greer against the Ohio Troops as they were more fearful of them than the Indians."[125]

The following day, Lieutenant Bretney received orders confirming Captain Greer's command of the fort. In addition, Major Martin Anderson, also of the Eleventh Kansas, was to command the entire district with his headquarters at Platte Bridge Station. As can be imagined, this situation further deteriorated the relationship between the Eleventh Kansas and Eleventh Ohio troops stationed at the bridge.[126]

While Platte Bridge Station was dealing with the mechanics of changing command, young Lieutenant Caspar Collins was just leaving his post at Sweetwater Station to head to Fort Laramie to obtain new horses for his men. Lieutenant Bretney gave Collins permission to spend a few extra days at Fort Laramie while sending his men back with their new mounts. Outraged that Collins had not returned to Platte Bridge with his men, General Connor accused him of being a coward and ordered him to return at once. Caspar Collins set out in his new uniform he had just ordered at Fort Laramie with the mail ambulance under Corporal Paul

Major Martin Anderson, Eleventh Kansas Cavalry. *Kansas State Historical Society*.

This picture, taken in 1868 at Fort Laramie, depicts Old-Man-[Be]-Afraid-of-His-Horses (standing between the two seated men in the center). *Wyoming State Archives, Department of State Parks and Cultural Resources.*

Grimm and ten men of the Eleventh Kansas. The party left Fort Laramie on July 22.[127]

On roughly the same day, a war council was held between a large number of Sioux and Cheyenne warriors. Present were George Bent (a half-Cheyenne man), Oglala, Miniconjou, Brule, Sans Arc, Northern and Southern Cheyenne and Arapaho, whose lodges numbered around one thousand. The chiefs chose Platte Bridge Station to be the target of a major attack in the hopes of taking over the post. According to Bent, nearly three thousand warriors headed toward the fort in a line stretching about two miles. The Cheyenne were led by Dull Knife, White Bull and Roman Nose. The Sioux were led by infamous chief Red Cloud, Old Man [Be] Afraid of His Horses and Young Man [Be] Afraid of His Horses. The Foolish Dogs encircled the band and were given the task of making sure that all warriors stuck to the plan and did not attack too soon. On the evening of July 24, they stopped to camp about six miles from the fort. Keeping with tradition on the eve of battle, the chiefs did not permit any singing in camp that night.[128]

George Bent and his wife, Magpie. *University of Colorado–Boulder Libraries.*

Sioux chief Red Cloud, taken in 1900. *Library of Congress.*

The soldiers at Platte Bridge Station could not possibly have been aware of the sheer size of the attack that was about to befall them. This was the largest war party ever organized to attack the small post that numbered fewer than 150 men. Major Anderson's reaction to this attack remains controversial to this day, and Caspar Collins would go on to become the city of Casper's most famous resident and namesake.

Chapter 3

BATTLES OF PLATTE BRIDGE STATION AND RED BUTTES

The summer of 1865 was fraught with tension between Native American tribes and the military. Each side was carrying on a campaign of revenge against the other, often as a result of perceived slights or legitimate atrocities. The soldiers of Platte Bridge Station fell under attack for offenses they personally did not commit; they were attacked simply because they were military personnel and represented the United States government.

The strategy of the Native Americans was the same that they had been using throughout their attacks: send a small party of decoys to draw the soldiers out of the post and then lead them into an ambush where the soldiers would be overwhelmed by their superior numbers. The chiefs sent a party of ten warriors down a small creek that ran by the fort. Their job was to attract the attention of the soldiers and then draw them to a large hill to the north where the rest of the tribes were waiting to attack.[129]

At approximately 1:00 p.m. on July 25, 1865, the soldiers of Platte Bridge Station noticed a party of about twenty warriors near the fort on the bluffs. A small detachment of Eleventh Kansas men was ordered to drive them off. As the detachment pursued the Sioux three miles away from the bridge, more warriors began to join them until there were approximately forty Sioux involved in the skirmish. Lieutenant William Drew of Company I described the strategy of the Sioux to a newspaper several years later, writing that "their [Sioux] maneuvering had been for the purpose of leading our men as far away from all support as possible, and then to wipe them out by

Portrait of an Eleventh Ohio Cavalry soldier taken at Deer Creek Station. *Wyoming State Archives, Department of State Parks and Cultural Resources.*

superior numbers."[130] The tribes used this same strategy the following day to disastrous effect.

By 4:00 p.m., Lieutenant Caspar Collins had returned to the post from his journey to Fort Laramie with the mail ambulance. He reported seeing warriors trying to run off the cattle herd two miles to the east. Captain Greer took sixteen men of Company I, Caspar Collins and Corporal Grimm's squad, for a total of about thirty men, to run off the Native Americans. The soldiers succeeded in killing a Cheyenne chief, High-Backed Wolf, but suffered no casualties themselves. One soldier had been cut by a sabre by a warrior and another had been grazed on the hand by a Minié ball bullet. All in all, the troops made out relatively unscathed. Major Anderson ordered the men who had been sleeping outside the post's walls in tents to move inside the fort for safety.[131]

That evening, as the men were in good spirits after their success during the day, Major Anderson discovered that the post was in dire need of ammunition. There were fewer than twenty rounds per man left for the Smith carbines (used by the Eleventh Kansas), and the situation was not any better for the other weapons. The men at the post had been making do with the ammunition issued to them when they had left Fort Riley the previous winter. Although they had requested ammunition from Fort Laramie, it had not yet arrived. Unbeknownst to the post, a wagon carrying the requested ammunition had left Fort Laramie and was on its way to them but would arrive too late to be of any help in the current situation. Faced with the possibility of another attack, the men began quickly making more ammunition.[132]

That same day, Lieutenant Bretney's detail and Sergeant Custard's supply train arrived at Sweetwater Station. As soon as the party had finished unloading its wagons, it started its return trip back to Platte Bridge. The men camped for the evening about twenty-five miles from the fort and midway between the two outposts. After Custard and his wagon train had left Sweetwater Station, Bretney received a telegram that his company's pay had arrived in Fort Laramie and that he should come immediately to pick it up. He left that afternoon with Captain A. Smyth Lybe of the Third U.S. Volunteer Infantry (who also was required to pick up pay) and found Custard's wagon train camped at Willow Springs. Bretney urged Custard to return to Platte Bridge with him, but the sergeant refused, saying that his animals were too tired and that they would return in the morning once the animals had rested. Bretney also informed Custard that he had received intelligence that various tribes were camped in the area, but Custard seemed unfazed by the information and refused to move. Bretney and Lybe continued on their journey, leaving Custard behind at approximately 9:00 p.m.[133]

Arriving at Platte Bridge at 2:00 a.m. on July 26, Bretney hurried into Major Anderson's room, woke him and pleaded for him to issue orders forcing Sergeant Custard to return to the post immediately. Unmoved, Anderson chose to go back to sleep and issued no such orders. Frustrated and convinced of an impending attack, Bretney had his men put their horses in the corral and their bedding in the square of the compound so that they could be ready for action at a moment's notice.[134]

In the early morning hours, the large war party of Sioux, Cheyenne and Arapaho warriors still lay undiscovered by the troops. The warriors had sent a party to split themselves into two main positions on either side of the river, east of the post. The Oglala chief Crazy Horse and Charlie Bent (George Bent's brother) were hidden in this location. Roman Nose and the Dog Soldiers were hidden behind some small bluffs west of the bridge by the river. They had effectively trapped anyone going into or out of the fort on the road. A large party of warriors remained camped behind the big hill with George Bent.[135]

Infamous Cheyenne chief and warrior Roman Nose. *Kansas State Historical Society.*

On the morning of July 26, the garrison of Platte Bridge Station included 70 men of Company I, Eleventh Kansas; 3 men of Company H, Eleventh Kansas; 14 men of Company K, Third U.S. Infantry; and Sergeant Hervey G. Merwin of Company G, Eleventh Ohio, and 3 men manning the mountain howitzer. The arrival of the detachments of Corporal Grimm from the east with 10 men of Company K, Eleventh Kansas; Lieutenant Bretney, with 10 men of Company G, Eleventh Ohio; and Captain Lybe of the Third Infantry, and the arrival of Caspar Collins, increased the number to 119 officers and men. The majority of the men were equipped with rifles, while the Eleventh Kansas soldiers were issued Smith single-shot carbines and the Eleventh Ohio soldiers used seven-shot Spencer repeating carbines.[136]

That morning, Lieutenant Bretney offered to retrieve Sergeant Custard if he was given a large number of men and the use of the howitzer. Major Anderson would not agree to send seventy to one hundred men as Bretney had requested, as that would have severely depleted the manpower at the fort itself. He did agree, however, to send twenty men to find Sergeant Custard. Bretney refused to lead such a small number of men out of the post and considered the job a suicide mission. No one from the Eleventh Kansas volunteered to lead the party for the same reasons as Bretney's refusal. The Kansans were also due to muster out of service in about two weeks and saw no reason to risk their lives unless absolutely necessary.[137]

This is an important moment in the history of the Eleventh Kansas and Eleventh Ohio at the post. Today, the men of the Eleventh Kansas are often excluded or misrepresented as cowards because they did not volunteer for this mission. This slanted opinion has its roots in the research of early local historians in the 1920s who idolized both Caspar Collins and the Eleventh Ohio. Several of them received the vast majority of their information from Bretney's son and did not compensate for the natural bias in information between a father and son. In this instance, it is important to point out that the Eleventh Kansas held a respectable war record and had just been involved in a skirmish the day prior.

At dawn, a large number of Native Americans was seen on the hilltop to the north, and Major Anderson decided that someone needed to find Sergeant Custard's wagon train. He summoned Lieutenant Caspar Collins to his office and ordered him to take a party of twenty troops to locate Sergeant Custard's detachment and bring it back to the post immediately. Collins, who had previously volunteered to go if given more men, objected to the size of the detachment he was to lead. The major asked him if he was refusing to obey his orders, to which he replied that he always followed his orders and promptly left the office. It is likely that Anderson did not want to send Captain Greer, as he had already skirmished the day before, and his other officers were on sick leave or unavailable. He could not send Captain Lybe because his men were only equipped with single-shot muskets, which would have been ineffective in an ambush.[138] At that time, Major Anderson and the fort would have been unaware of the numbers of warriors hidden around the post, and although it did certainly seem like a suicide mission, Major Anderson knew something had to be done. Given the situation, Lieutenant Collins was the logical choice to lead the detachment. This created the controversial situation of Lieutenant Caspar Collins of the Eleventh Ohio leading a detachment of Eleventh Kansas men.[139]

As for Major Anderson's decision not to send more troops per Bretney's request, it is likely that he did not feel that the fort would be sufficiently protected with only nineteen men (including himself). It is important to point out that Lieutenant Walker, who was present at the battle, wrote a lengthy defense of Major Anderson many years later. In it, he pointed out that Major Anderson sent double the guard with Caspar Collins than what was usual and required by Fort Laramie. He also was quick to point out that the post was so short of ammunition that Major Anderson had ordered him to purchase lead and powder from a ranch close to the post (likely Guinard's). In addition, he wrote that all the regimental staff officers of the Eleventh Kansas (excluding the surgeon) had already been ordered to Fort Leavenworth to muster out. Walker concluded by writing, "Major Anderson did all that any officer under the circumstances could do."[140]

No photo exists of Caspar Collins as a young man. This age progression image was created by SketchCop Solutions, LLC. *Fort Caspar Museum.*

Had Major Anderson sent men out during the night when Bretney first approached him about the matter, he may have been more successful and could have sent more men. However, it is likely that he feared an attack on the post, and his first duty was to the post.

Another issue often brought up is that Major Anderson supposedly had no right to send Caspar Collins of the Eleventh Ohio to lead the rescue effort since he was not permanently assigned to the post and was simply passing through on his way back to Sweetwater Station. In fact, Caspar Collins was assigned to a subpost of Platte Bridge Station. Even though Lieutenant Collins was not based there, as the commander of that district, Major Anderson was within his rights to order him to lead the detachment.

Lieutenant Bretney urged Collins not to go and tried to convince him to disobey his orders. Collins could not be dissuaded from his orders despite the fact that he was not comfortable with what he was about to do. He borrowed Bretney's set of Colt pistols and was forced to borrow a horse, as his horse was back at Sweetwater Station. The horse that he rode had a reputation for being difficult and unwieldy when excited. Still, he had no other option and rode out on the large iron gray animal.[141]

Anderson had instructed Collins not to ride on the main road but to ride north to the top of the hill and turn west until he met up with the road that would lead him to Custard's wagons. Anderson wanted him to remain in line of sight from the fort, and being at the top of the hill would also give Collins visibility to the north if hostiles were to approach. Bretney, still angry over the fact that Collins had been sent on this mission, stormed into Major Anderson's office, telling him that "it was not in his province to send Collins out since he had some of his own officers present for duty."[142] Anderson dismissed Bretney and told him to mind his own business. Bretney, of course, was upset that a Kansan commander had sent an Eleventh Ohio officer (and his close friend) into battle when there were Kansan officers available for duty. What Bretney failed to take into account, and Major Anderson did, was that those Kansan troops had fought an engagement the previous day and that, as commander of the post, he could send whomever he wanted into battle, regardless of what state they were from. Still, this situation played right into the already growing resentment between the Kansas and Ohio troops.[143]

At about 7:30 a.m., Collins rode out in his brand-new uniform with Bretney's pistols stuffed in his boots and a cigar in his mouth. Not long after the column had crossed the bridge, Lieutenant Walker spotted two groups of warriors south of the road and on the west bank of the river. "Major Anderson ordered twenty men under Bretney and Lybe to follow Collins' column on foot in order to protect his rear."[144] Bretney had ten men with him, while Lybe came up with an additional fourteen infantrymen. Some traders, trappers and other civilians who had been camping at the bridge joined in the line to help defend Collins and the post as best as they could. The men were also ordered to be mindful of their shooting, as ammunition was in very short supply and they could not afford to waste it.[145]

As soon as Collins and his column reached the top of the hill as instructed, they came across two warriors who had climbed the telegraph pole and were cutting wires. Collins ordered his men to attack, and as they charged toward

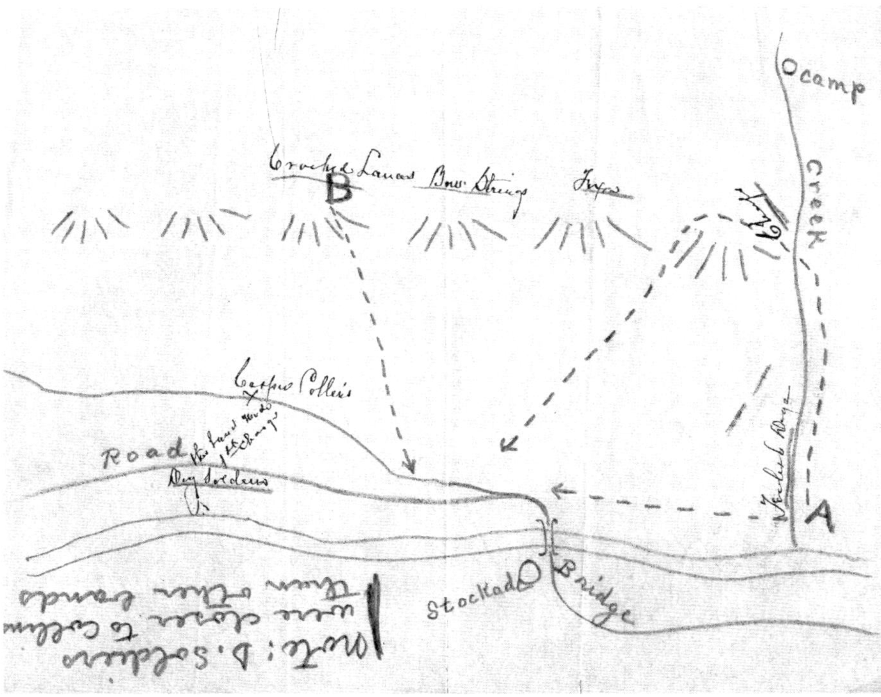

This seldom-seen map comes from George Bent and depicts the positions of the various Native American tribes during the Battle of Platte Bridge. *University of Colorado–Boulder Libraries.*

the telegraph pole, they disappeared from the view of the fort. At that moment, about four hundred Cheyenne warriors led by Big Horse emerged seemingly out of nowhere and charged at Collins. In response, Collins ordered his men by fours into line in order to meet the Cheyenne coming up from the riverbank. This maneuver left Collins in the rear of his troops. This, combined with the nature of the ground, created a situation of poor visibility in which Collins could not see other warriors approaching until it was too late. The rest of the Cheyenne and Sioux came out of cover and surrounded the small detachment. The soldiers were forced to ride forward into the mass of warriors in order to return to the bridge.[146] Sergeant Jake (Isaac) Pennock, Company L, Eleventh Kansas, recalled, "We turned and charged in the thickest of them, drawing our pistols and doing the best we could. It was a terrible ordeal to go through. It really was running the gauntlet for dear life."[147]

Due to the large masse of Native Americans attacking simultaneously, the warriors chose not to use their firearms for fear of killing too many of their own. Instead, they attacked with lances, sabers and other handheld

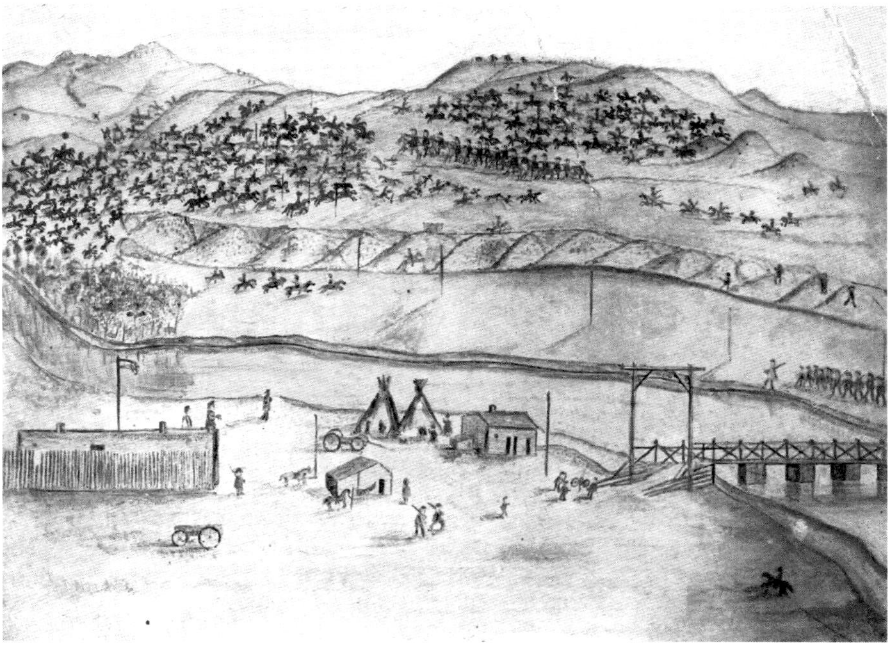

An illustration of the Battle of Platte Bridge. Notice Caspar Collins's detachment overwhelmed by Native Americans in the top center and the reinforcements led by Captain Greer just leaving the bridge on the middle right edge. *Kansas State Historical Society*.

weapons. When they did fire at Collins's detachment, they tended to fire high and thus missed many of the men. As Collins's detachment rode at breakneck speed for the bridge, supposedly one of Collins's men's horses was struck clean through by a bullet, which knocked the soldier to the ground. As he called for help, Collins, who had already been wounded in the hip, turned back to help his fallen comrade. At that point, his horse, which by some reports was unstable, spooked in all the commotion and galloped straight toward Dry Creek to the northeast. Although the Sioux recognized Collins as a friend, the Cheyenne did not and shot arrows at him as he struggled to regain control of his horse. George Bent, who was fighting on the side of the Sioux, Cheyenne and Arapaho, remembered "an arrow sticking in his forehead and his face…streaming with blood."[148] Lieutenant Caspar Collins tumbled down from the top of the hill, dead.

The death of Caspar Collins is significant because the story has been told and retold with varying degrees of accuracy. George Bent's description is important because he claims that Collins was already dead when his horse spooked and ran toward his attackers. This casts doubt on the more romantic story of young Lieutenant Collins making a valiant charge to the death. The exaggerated version of the story is that Caspar Collins was galloping back to the post when he heard the cries of a wounded comrade, Adam Culp of the Eleventh Ohio, and turned sharply around to attempt to help him. He picked Culp up and propped him across his saddle in front of him, and while doing so, his horse spooked and Culp fell off. His horse took him back into the fray, at which point he put the reins of his horse between his teeth, pulled out the two pistols Bretney had given him and rode off valiantly to his death with a Colt in each hand.[149] Unfortunately, this romantic story has some factual errors, the first being that Adam Culp was not in fact with Caspar Collins at that moment. He was with Custard's wagon train, which had not yet come under attack.[150] The second problem is that George Bent clearly describes Caspar Collins with an arrow wound to the head at the time his horse took off running. This would mean that Lieutenant Collins was dead before his horse ran back into the battle. In fact, his horse may have taken off running due to the fact that Collins had died and was no longer in control of it. At the very minimum, this story is wrong with regard to the name of the soldier requesting Collins's aid for help. However, it is more likely that the story was highly exaggerated or outright invented by Collins's mourning comrades and newspapers eager for a fantastic story. Whether or not Collins knowingly charged into the midst of his attackers does not diminish his bravery or sacrifice for his country. Given the chaos on the battlefield at the time of his death, it is unlikely that the exact circumstances of his death will ever be known.

After Collins's death, the rest of his detachment struggled to make it back to the bridge, with varying success. Private Frederick Erhardt described the scene to a Kansas newspaper many years later. Galloping toward the post, he remembered, "There was no time to reload. I dropped my carbine on the sling to my side and drew my revolver, pointing it at one, then another, then another, which had the effect to make them dodge right and left."[151] By most accounts it was mass confusion, but a few of the men were lucky enough to make it to safety.

Corporal Grimm returned to the post following Erhardt but had several arrow wounds to his back. Cover fire provided by Lieutenant Bretney, Captain Lybe and the ragtag group of civilians allowed all but four others to return safely to the post. Sergeant Merwin fired the howitzer as the beleaguered troopers raced back to the fort in an effort to scatter the warriors who were chasing them. He could not fire the howitzer during much of the engagement out of fear of hitting his own troops. Captain Greer "was

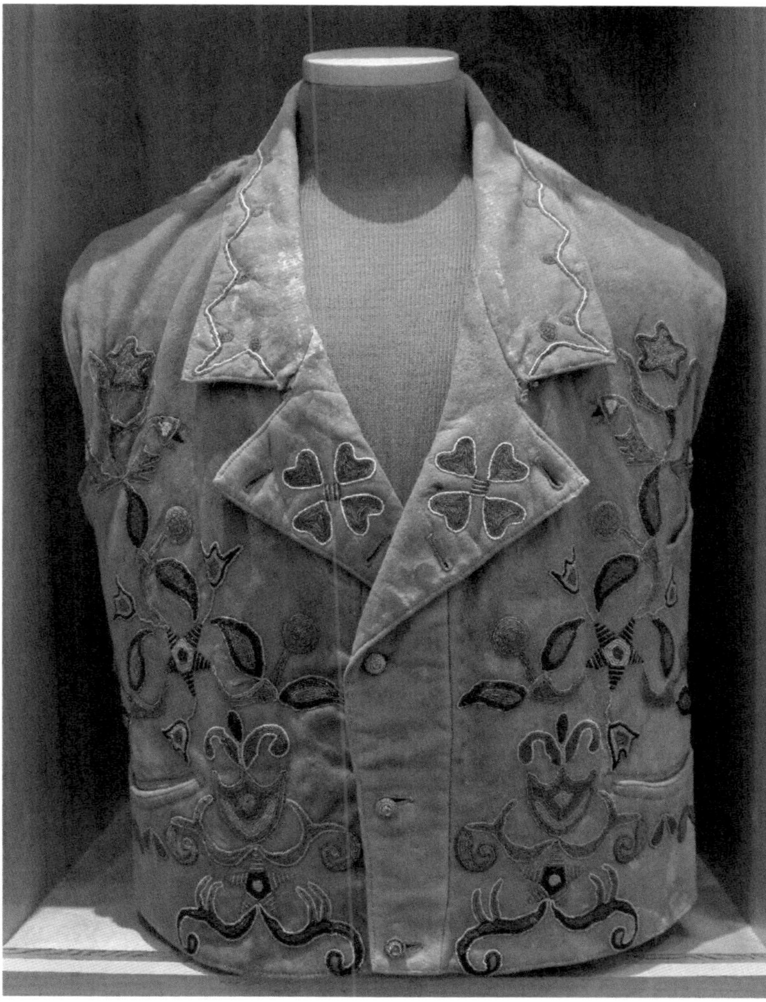

This decorative vest once belonged to Caspar Collins. *Fort Caspar Museum.*

present everywhere, encouraging by command presence the men whose confidence he possessed and whom he knew would stand as long, and in any place he would direct."[152]

John Hart of the Eleventh Kansas recalled that many of the Native Americans who had participated in the attack remained on a mesa near the fort within firing range of the howitzer. Although the battle was over, the fort's howitzer fired several shells at the gloating warriors. The shells turned out to be duds, however, as they simply struck the earth and rolled around a bit. Hart recalled, "Finally we shot one shell that rolled over the mesa and as

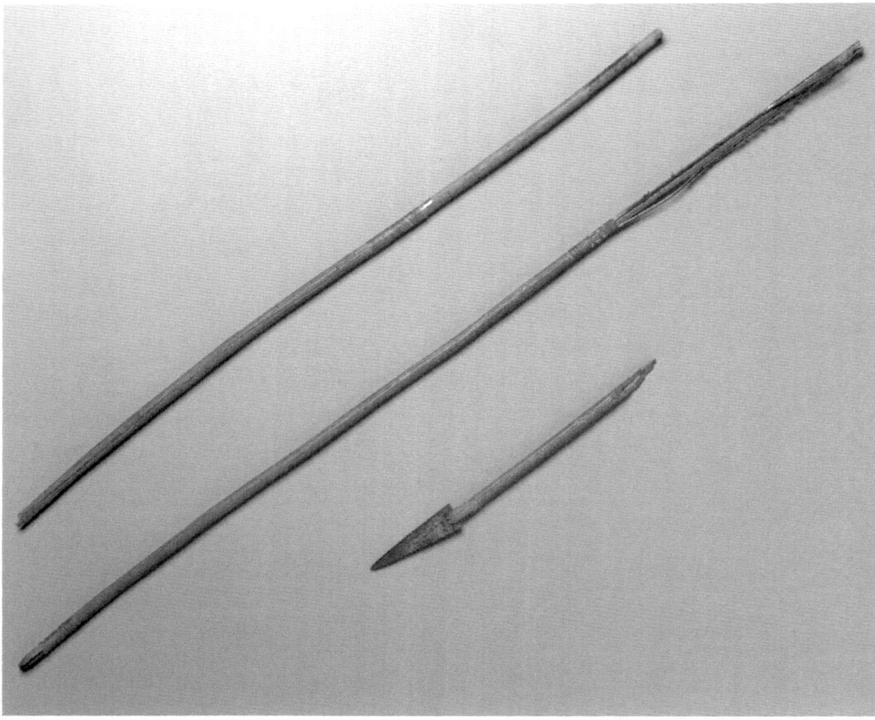

This never-before-seen photo shows the arrows pulled from Corporal Grimm's back. *Kansas State Historical Society*.

usual a bunch of Indians ran after it, and after it became still for probably three minutes it exploded killing three Indians."[153]

A friendly Shoshoni scout rode into the post to inform the command that he had witnessed the Sioux and Cheyenne chiefs arguing among themselves for not taking the bridge as had been planned and for shooting over the heads of Collins's men and only wounding many of them. The Battle of Platte Bridge, as it came to be called, was over in a period of only thirty to sixty minutes. In addition to Caspar Collins, Privates George W. McDonald and Sebastian Nehring of Company I, Eleventh Kansas, and Privates George Camp and Moses Brown of Company H, Eleventh Kansas, were killed in action. Sergeant Adolph Hankammer, Corporal Henry Grimm and Privates Henry W. Hill, Jesse Playford, Benjamin P. Goddard, George D. May, Harley L. Stoddard, Harvey Craven and Andrew Baker were wounded. The majority of men came from Company I, Eleventh Kansas, except for Hankammer (who was in Company K, Eleventh Kansas) and Baker (Company L, Eleventh Kansas).

The rescue attempt to save Custard's wagon train had failed horrifically due to the overwhelming numbers of 2,500 to 3,000 Native American warriors involved.[154] In retrospect, it was very lucky that any of Collins's detachment survived at all.

At 9:00 a.m., Lieutenant George Walker and seventeen men along with Captain Lybe and ten infantrymen were sent to repair the telegraph line about two miles east of the post. Major Anderson had given them new signals that would warn them if danger approached. A flag would be waved at the fort if Native Americans were nearby, and the howitzer would be fired as a signal for them to return to the post immediately.[155] Half an hour later, Major Anderson called a meeting in his office with Lieutenant Bretney and Captain Greer. "Knowing that Collins had been lost, Bretney confronted the major, accusing him of murder and telling him in blunt language that he was unfit to command. Greer became involved in the argument, and Bretney struck him."[156] Bretney was immediately placed in confinement but released six hours later. Throughout his confinement, he still offered to rescue Custard if given one hundred men and the howitzer. Major Anderson, of course, declined his offer.[157]

Lieutenant Walker and Captain Lybe were soon under attack as they attempted to repair the telegraph line. Shortly after beginning work, the men heard the howitzer and immediately began their retreat to the fort. While the men retreated, some troopers of Company I came out of the fort to cover their comrades. While Walker and Lybe's detachment was heading back to the post, Custard's wagon train had finally come into view of the fort, about four miles out. Unfortunately, as the train had just become visible to the soldiers of Platte Bridge Station, it had also become visible to the Cheyenne and Sioux warriors nearby.[158]

At about 11:00 a.m., large numbers of Sioux and Cheyenne warriors descended on Custard's wagon train. Custard had planned to move the wagons to higher ground on a rise a few hundred yards away but was unable to get his mules to move quickly enough, so he was forced to circle his wagons and fight where he was. This placed Custard and his men down in a hollow, which made them far more vulnerable to attack. Reports vary from between two and five wagons in Custard's party. The fight took place in plain view of Platte Bridge Station, and the majority of observers at the post seem to agree that there were three wagons arranged in such a way that they were positioned to the north, east and south, leaving the western side open in a sideways *u* formation.[159]

Corporal Shrader had been ordered by Custard to move ahead and organize a force to meet the attack. In doing so, he became cut off from the rest of

Sergeant Amos Custard, Eleventh Kansas Cavalry. *Kansas State Historical Society*.

Custard's wagon train. He joined Privates Henry Smith, Byron Swain, Edwin Summers and James Ballau, and they made a break for the river to the right. Upon crossing the river, Summers became separated from the group and was last seen heading toward the foothills of Casper Mountain. Ballau was killed immediately after crossing the river. Shrader abandoned his horse and ran to catch up to Smith and Swain, who had ridden across the plain and hidden in a deep ravine covered with brush. They moved along in this ravine for about half

Painting by William Henry Jackson depicting the Battle of Red Buttes. *Scottsbluff National Monument.*

a mile before making a run for another gulch that took them closer to the fort. While running to the gulch, they were seen by troopers at the fort, and twenty men went out to meet them. Another twenty warriors chased the three men, but they were able to make it to Platte Bridge Station alive. They were the only survivors of Custard's wagon train massacre.[160]

Custard's wagon train was fully surrounded, and their attempts to repulse their attackers were futile. According to George Bent, the Sioux and Cheyenne fired almost continually into the circled wagons in order to force the soldiers into exhausting their ammunition by firing back. Once they determined that the soldiers' ammunition was low, they stormed the wagons and killed all the occupants.[161]

By 4:00 p.m., the gunshots coming from the wagon train had stopped, and soon smoke was seen coming from that location as the warriors began burning the wagons. A small party left at 5:00 p.m. from the post to search for the dead but quickly drew the attention of surrounding tribes. Bretney, who had just been released from confinement, was only able to retrieve one body, that of Private Moses Brown, who was buried that evening at the post.[162]

Speculations vary as to the number of Native American casualties from the battles. Many soldiers stated that the warriors did not keep the scalps that they took, which was a sign that they had lost more of their own than they had killed. One Native American claimed a loss of 200 warriors, while George Bent claimed that only 8 warriors died. Another source claimed that 60 Native Americans had been killed and around 130 wounded.[163] "Including the deaths of Private Porter in Walker's command and the four enlisted men of the 11th Kansas with Collins, the total casualties on July 26 were one officer and one enlisted man of the 11th Ohio and twenty-six men of the 11th Kansas killed and nine or ten men wounded."[164]

The next morning, the tribes taunted the men at the fort, claiming that they had killed Caspar Collins and were soon going to murder all of them as well and burn the fort to the ground. The ammunition situation was extremely dire at the bridge, and fearing another attack, Anderson ordered the men to gather what powder and lead they could from the civilians camped at the post in order to make more cartridges. By 8:00 a.m., the warriors largely seemed to have left the area after destroying about five miles of telegraph line. By 3:00 p.m., the men at Platte Bridge were elated at the arrival of fifty men of the Eleventh Kansas under Lieutenant Josiah Hubbard from Deer Creek and five thousand rounds of ammunition.[165]

According to one of the men who retrieved Caspar Collins's body, "warriors had driven twenty-four arrows into the body, which had been wrapped in telegraph wire. Collins had been stripped naked, the back part of his head caved in, the brains taken out, the heart and bowels taken out, and the feet and hands cut off."[166] The bodies of Sebastian Nehring and George McDonald were also found that day. They had also been severely mutilated. McDonald's legs had been severed and tied to his corpse with telegraph wire. Nehring's hands were cut off and his tongue and heart removed.[167]

The scene at Custard's wagons was even more gruesome. Twenty-five men went out to locate the bodies and bury them in a mass grave at the site. Jake Pennock was with the party and remembered "seventeen of Custard's men lying upon their faces, their naked, mutilated bodies pinioned to the ground with long spears. All had been scalped, but one. A wagoner was strapped to his feed-box, and hot irons from the hubs of the wagon wheels had been placed along his back."[168] Lieutenant Drew described the man as having had "a wagon tire laid across his bowels."[169] Pennock wrote in his diary, "A horrible sight…the bodies nearly all burned up. The savages set fire to the wagons and heated iron bolts and burned the men with them and turned their feet to the fire torturing them alive in every possible manner."[170] Adam Culp, the only member of the Eleventh Ohio with the group, was tied to a wagon wheel and had been tortured with a hot skillet on his back. The charred remains of one man were among the coals of a burned wagon. Other soldiers noticed that Custard's men had been seemingly tortured with other hot metal items. Other reports mention mutilation, similar to what had befallen Caspar Collins and those who had been killed with him.[171] The bodies were buried in two mass graves, seven in one and thirteen in the other.[172] No coffins were used, as the men were laid to rest in three-foot trenches covered with rubber blankets.[173]

Upon notification of his son's death, Colonel William O. Collins ordered an investigation into the conduct of Major Anderson. A court of inquiry at Fort Laramie began on April 7, 1866, with only members of the Eleventh Ohio, and it did not hear any testimony from those actually involved in the battle.[174] As could be expected, the board of inquiry sided with Colonel Collins of the Eleventh Ohio rather than Major Anderson of the Eleventh Kansas. The board decided that it was out of Anderson's command to order young Caspar Collins to command a detachment of Eleventh Kansas troops when officers from the Eleventh Kansas were available and that Anderson did not clearly have the authority to order Caspar Collins to go on this mission since he was not stationed at the post. The board also agreed that Anderson should have sent relief out to Collins after seeing the large war party on the ridge swooping down on him. Lastly, in order to have avoided the entire situation, the board decided that Anderson should have sent relief to Custard the evening before when Lieutenant Bretney first reported seeing the wagon train.[175]

However, it is unlikely that Custard would have budged from his spot considering all the pleading that Bretney had done that night and he still declined to move. In addition, that night, Anderson had no way of knowing the size of the Native American war party. Hindsight is always 20/20, and given the hatred between the Eleventh Ohio and Eleventh Kansas, it is easy to see why Colonel Collins would be quick to blame Major Anderson. George Walker of the Eleventh Kansas later wrote that the shortage of ammunition at the post may have been largely to blame for Major Anderson's seemingly weak response to saving the Custard wagon train. The ammunition supply was so low that Major Anderson had directed Walker to procure any lead and powder he could from the civilians camped nearby in order to hastily make cartridges for the defense of the fort. Walker later wrote, "Had we not been short of ammunition I have reason to believe a greater effort could have been made to rescue Sergeant Custard's command."[176] The army suffered heavy casualties, but given the number of warriors involved in the attack, nearly any strategy other than simply remaining at the post would have been futile.

Fort Caspar Closes

In early August 1865, the troops of the Eleventh Kansas were officially mustered out of service. Lieutenant Colonel Plumb had been promoted to colonel but was mustered out of service before the paperwork could be finished.[177] Platte Bridge Station had a new commander, Major Andrew Squires of West Virginia. The garrison at the post varied between 184 and 360 men from West Virginia and Ohio.[178]

That November, Platte Bridge Station was officially renamed Fort Caspar in honor of Caspar Collins. Traditionally, the renaming of a fort would use the person's last name, but there was already a Fort Collins named after Caspar's father.[179]

By winter, food and clean water were in scarce supply. The troops were running out of vegetables, tobacco, tea and ammunition. The first bridge crossing in the area, Richard's Bridge, was scavenged for wood, and pieces were brought back to the post to use as firewood. The men at the post now faced a new threat much worse than the dreaded Native American attack: disease. During the winter, scurvy broke out among the men. The cause, as determined by Surgeon Dryden, was the lack of vegetables. He worried that the disease would spread to more soldiers if he could not institute some form of fruit or vegetables into the men's diets. Luckily, in March, wagons filled with dried fruits and vegetables arrived at the post from Fort Laramie, and there were no further scurvy outbreaks.[180]

The winter that had been so hard on the troops stationed at Fort Caspar was even harder on the Native American tribes. On March 1, 1866, the garrison at Fort Laramie was surprised to see a band of Brule Sioux led by Chief Standing Elk waving a white blanket of surrender. Standing Elk complained that his people were starving and that they were unable to hunt buffalo, antelope and deer because the "white soldier" had killed them all. He brought his tribe to Fort Laramie in order to negotiate peace.[181] Standing Elk had brought his entire tribe of well over five hundred to the fort, and they were promptly fed as they turned their firearms in to the fort's commander. Not long after that, another 150 lodges of Sioux and 90 Arapaho lodges were captured by General Mitchell. That summer, a peace council was held at Fort Laramie with about seven thousand Native Americans and their most prominent chiefs in attendance. In June 1866, many of the tribes that had been responsible for the attacks in and around Fort Caspar signed the treaty.[182]

General William T. Sherman (third from left) meeting with Native American chiefs and commissioners at Fort Laramie for the Treaty of Fort Laramie in 1868. *Wyoming State Archives, Department of State Parks and Cultural Resources.*

Also that month, Fort Caspar received a new commander, Captain Richard Morris. Immediately, he and his men of the Eighteenth Infantry began work on repairing and improving the buildings at Fort Caspar. A reporter from Salt Lake City visited the post that summer and wrote that the soldiers were busy making improvements to the fort in order to garrison as many as five hundred men, which would make it nearly the same size as Fort Laramie.[183] Although that had originally been the plan, developments in Native American relations had minimized the need for the outpost, let alone enlarging it. By January 1867, the Pacific Telegraph line, which the men had been protecting, switched to an alternate route, and suddenly there was no need for small outposts every thirty to fifty miles protecting a line no longer in use. The smaller outposts such as St. Mary's, Sweetwater and South Pass were closed, and the troops were withdrawn.[184]

Red Cloud's war with the army took the focus to northern Wyoming and consequently drew the Native Americans away from the mail routes between Fort Caspar and Fort Laramie.[185] By the spring of 1867, the garrison at Fort Caspar had a few small entanglements with Native Americans but nothing

Reconstructed officers' quarters at Fort Caspar Museum. *Author's collection.*

on the scale of the Battle of Platte Bridge. As summer came, the fighting against the Sioux and Cheyenne shifted north, closer to the Bozeman Trail. The fall of 1867 signaled another major event in the decline of the fort: the construction of the railroad. The Union Pacific Railroad crossed through the southern half of the state in Cheyenne, over two hundred miles from Fort Caspar. In response, the army shifted its focus from protecting overland trails to protecting the railroad. On October 19, 1867, the adjutant general ordered Fort Caspar to be abandoned. Any and all materials that could be reused were hauled to build the new post, Fort Fetterman, on La Prele Creek, near the present-day city of Douglas.[186]

Louis Guinard abandoned his bridge at Fort Caspar at roughly the same time. Shortly after leaving, some Arapaho and Northern Cheyenne burned his bridge to the ground. Guinard ended up working as an interpreter at Fort Washakie.[187]

The mission of Fort Caspar had been fulfilled. During its five-year operation, it protected travelers and the great telegraph line, so crucial to the country. Eventually, it was replaced by the railroad, and as the troubles with local tribes began to draw to a close, frontier outposts quickly became ghost towns.

CONCLUSION

The mission of these posts beginning in 1855 and concluding in 1867 was fairly simple: protect the trails, protect the telegraph lines and keep the peace. To that end, the men who were stationed here succeeded in their mission to the best of their abilities. Working under the cover of darkness in dangerous weather and with roaming hostile Native American tribes, these men, many of whom were only teenagers or in their early twenties, worked tirelessly to restore communication with the telegraph lines. Isolated and away from support from allies, officers were tasked with making snap decisions in order to avoid bloodshed with local tribes or to settle disputes among traders, travelers and Native Americans. Their time here was not without incident, and although there may be debate as to whether those situations could have been handled differently, there is no doubt that the men were under a tremendous amount of stress and acted as they saw fit.

Post at Platte Bridge came out of a need to protect travelers along the Oregon Trail, similar to the creation of its much larger compatriot, Fort Laramie. However, Post at Platte Bridge was designed and garrisoned with only enough men to protect the bridge crossing. There were no telegraph lines to protect at the time and no other neighboring outposts. During the post's second incarnation, it was reopened in order to protect Albert Sidney Johnston's supply lines during his Utah Expedition. Although the conflict had officially ended by the time the post reopened, it was still critical to ensure that the supplies traveling to the troops in Utah got to their destination unhindered by hostile Mormons or Native Americans. Post at Platte Bridge was successful in this mission, as there were no attacks on the post or missing supplies during its operation. Although the conflict may have been hundreds of miles away, a small outpost such as this played an important role in ensuring the success of Johnston's campaign.

Platte Bridge Station encompassed the same needs as Post at Platte Bridge in the sense that both were located at vital bridge crossings along the North Platte. Migrant traffic decreased during the Civil War, but tensions with Native American tribes increased, and the post was necessary in order to protect goods and supplies. In addition, Platte Bridge Station protected a telegraph office on site and also had oversight over the various smaller stations such as Rocky Ridge and Deer Creek. Platte Bridge Station was centrally located between the other stations and could efficiently send soldiers to the other stations if needed for repairs. The distances between the posts were too great to offer any military protection from the main station, so small detachments of soldiers were sent out to the outposts to help defend them against Native American attacks.

Camp Dodge only existed for a couple months and would have been set up similar to any other battlefield encampment during the Civil War. As regimental headquarters for the Eleventh Kansas Cavalry, it would have included as many as one hundred men and possibly moved slightly in the area as the horses began to graze through the grass. The purpose of Camp Dodge was similar to Platte Bridge Station in that they both provided oversight of the smaller telegraph outposts along the line and sent small detachments of men to protect and repair the stations as necessary. The main difference was that Camp Dodge did not have a telegraph office on site to protect or a bridge crossing. Camp Dodge's location was high enough in the hills to oversee Platte Bridge Station and provide a lookout should the station come under attack. Since Camp Dodge was a tent encampment, there were no sturdy structures to protect the men, and it was eventually abandoned in favor of garrisoning the men at Platte Bridge Station, where the wood and earthen buildings offered some protection from attack.

All three outposts played important roles in larger national conflicts and events, whether it was the large migration along the westward trails, Johnston's Utah Expedition, the Civil War or the Plains Indian Wars. By keeping communication open via telegraph and mail, ensuring travelers' safety or maintaining the peace whenever possible with local Native American tribes, these posts were invaluable to the country's history.

Post at Platte Bridge has been neglected in many historical works of the region, and this book sheds new light on the significance of the post and the commanding officers. In 2014, the City of Evansville turned the historic location into a housing development, citing the fact that the military post was of no historical value. Unfortunately, this is the end result of a local lack of knowledge of the site. While no major skirmishes took place at the post, the horrific instance of Fire Wolf's unjustified imprisonment and eventual death serves as a tragic reminder of the paranoia and carelessness with which human life was often treated on the frontier. The fact that two major historical figures—Henry Heth and Joseph Roberts—were in command of the post at some time also lends importance to the site.

The bulk of this book focuses on attempting to restore the reputation of the Eleventh Kansas Cavalry stationed at Camp Dodge and, later, Platte Bridge Station. The death of Caspar Collins has been romanticized throughout the years, which seems to have come at the expense of the Eleventh Kansas. The regiment is blamed for sending young Caspar Collins out on a virtual suicide mission, but these historians seem to neglect the fact that it was Major Anderson who sent Caspar Collins on this mission, not the entire Eleventh Kansas. Many historians call the Kansas officers cowards for not leading the charge, citing the fact that they were due to be mustered out soon. Yet they neglect to mention that the men who accompanied Caspar Collins were all Eleventh Kansas soldiers and that Captain Greer had just been involved in a skirmish the day prior.

Colonel Plumb of the Eleventh Kansas had nothing less than a spotless reputation as a commanding officer, and it is clear that his contributions were significant. While stationed in Wyoming, he was responsible for maintaining the operation of the telegraph and overland stage routes through his posts. "The Overland Company was astonished that communication was preserved. Colonel Plumb displayed so much ability in this work that Ben Holladay, owner of the Overland Company, urged him to retire from the army and become manager of the Overland lines from the Missouri River to the Pacific Coast."[188] He mustered out of the military in September 1865 and became a successful lawyer and banker. He served in the Kansas Statehouse in 1867 and 1868 before being elected to the U.S. Senate as a Republican in 1876. He continued to serve in the Senate until his death in 1891. Plumb was one of the most successful men stationed in the West and should be a household name in Wyoming.

Part of the reason for the neglect of the Eleventh Kansas in local history falls squarely on Lieutenant Bretney's shoulders. Bretney resented Major Anderson for sending his friend Caspar Collins on that mission and never fully recovered from Caspar's death. Even prior to that event, he had problems with the Eleventh Kansas, culminating in his drunken shooting incident in the summer of 1865. Although Bretney was eventually promoted to captain on September 28, 1865, he was tried in a court-martial the same day. He was accused of drinking while on duty and conduct unbecoming of an officer and a gentleman. He was found guilty and dismissed from the service on November 1.[189] Evidence suggests that in September 1867, Bretney reenlisted in the cavalry (Company B, Second Cavalry) under the assumed name of H.C. Brett. Brett deserted the service in July 1868.[190] Bretney's son, Henry Clay Bretney Jr., wished to write a book about his father's life but never completed it. In the process of writing his book, he communicated heavily with many historians and gave them his father's bitter version of events—which, of course, were biased heavily against the Eleventh Kansas. Many of these books became accepted locally as authorities on the subject, and Bretney's biased version of events has permeated throughout the city's local history. Interestingly, Bretney's court-martial is often excluded from those books.

Major Martin Anderson holds the most blame for the death of Caspar Collins. Had it not been for the Battle of Platte Bridge, it is likely that Major Anderson would have held a very good reputation within the army. Had he listened to Lieutenant Bretney when he burst into his quarters in the early morning hours and ordered Sergeant Custard to return to the post at once under the cover of darkness, the entire event may have been avoided. It is impossible to know for sure what actions the Native Americans would have taken, but it may have allowed Custard to return to the post undetected. By dawn on July 26, 1865, it was simply too late. Bretney's request for over 80 percent of the fort's manpower to accompany him on a rescue mission to Custard's wagon train was far too high to risk. When Major Anderson sent Caspar Collins out with his detachment, he had no way of knowing that three thousand warriors were waiting to attack. More than likely, he assumed it would be a war party of sixty to eighty warriors, as was often the case. In hindsight, knowing the numbers of the Native Americans' party, it is easy to characterize Casper Collins's mission as a suicide mission, but Major Anderson would not have known that at the time.

Most of the negativity toward Anderson comes from Lieutenant Bretney's information that he gave to his son. The rest of it comes from the board of inquiry held by Caspar Collins's father, Colonel William Collins. By any standard, the board was quite clearly a joke. It was composed entirely of Eleventh Ohio officers who did not interview a single member of the Eleventh Kansas (Anderson's regiment) or speak to anyone who was actually at the battle. From that, they drew their conclusions that Anderson never should have ordered Caspar Collins to leave the post. Of course, this verdict delighted Colonel Collins almost as if he had personally requested it. Had another officer led the charge without the military lineage of Caspar Collins, it is unlikely that there would have been any investigation at all. This was simply a case of a grieving father looking for someone to blame for his son's death. The inquiry had no effect on Major Anderson, as he was mustered out of the military the same time as Colonel Plumb and went on to be Kansas state treasurer for a number of years.[191]

Colonel William Collins mourned the death of his young son for the rest of his life. He remained angry at Major Anderson for ordering Caspar to lead that fateful detachment of Eleventh Kansas troopers into a Native American onslaught. Following his military career, he returned to his law practice and died in 1880.[192]

For Caspar Collins, perhaps the greatest sign of his legacy remains in the name of the city of Casper, Wyoming. Unfortunately, due to a clerical error, the city of Casper has the incorrect spelling, but regardless, it is no doubt named after young Caspar Collins.[193]

As the country reeled from the Great Depression of the 1930s, the Works Progress Administration chose to rebuild Fort Caspar on its original site as a

Fort Caspar today. *Author's collection.*

park and museum. The Civilian Conservation Corps began rebuilding the site in 1934 based off period drawings sketched by Caspar Collins. Wherever possible, the new structures were placed on their original foundations. By 1937, the newly reconstructed fort had become a popular tourist attraction, and a year later, workers discovered the remnants of Guinard's Bridge along with several graves still bearing the signs of their untimely deaths, with arrows protruding from the skeletons. Those that were found to be military graves were reburied at Fort Russell (F.E. Warren Air Force Base) in Cheyenne, Wyoming, along with a few of the other graves that had been reburied there in 1899.[194] The Fort Caspar Museum opened in 1983 and has since been remodeled. It continues to interpret the story of Fort Caspar and Louis Guinard.

Richard's and Guinard's bridges, and the subsequent military outposts, helped to establish the city of Casper as they drew migrants through the area and trappers and mountain men started to settle nearby. Subsequent mineral strikes and oil booms cemented the city of Casper as an important place within the state of Wyoming. Today, the city has upward of fifty-seven thousand people, but those men at Post at Platte Bridge and Fort Caspar were some of the first non–Native Americans to call this place home. Through their history and the remnants of their outposts and bridges, the city of Casper has a strong tie to the military history of the West.

NOTES

Introduction

1. Frazer, *Forts of the West*, 182.

Chapter 1

2. Murray, "Trading Posts," 7.
3. Church of Jesus Christ of Latter Day Saints, "Upper Platte (Mormon) Ferry."
4. Murray, "Trading Posts," 8.
5. McDermott, *Frontier Crossroads*, 8.
6. Ibid., 9.
7. Hemman, "Broken Promises," 2.
8. Glass, *Reshaw*, 95.
9. McDermott, *Frontier Crossroads*, 10.
10. William Hoffman to General Harney.
11. William Hoffman to Lieutenant Deshler.
12. McDermott, *Frontier Crossroads*, 10, 11.
13. Ibid., 11.
14. Monthly Returns, Post at Platte Bridge.
15. McDermott, *Frontier Crossroads*, 11.
16. Ibid.
17. Heth and Morrison, *Memoirs*, 133.

18. McDermott, *Frontier Crossroads*, 12.
19. Ibid., 12, 13.
20. Ibid., 13.
21. William Hoffman to Henry Heth.
22. William Hoffman to Captain Pleasanton.
23. William Hoffman to Thomas Twiss.
24. William Hoffman to Captain A.P. Howe.
25. McDermott, *Frontier Crossroads*, 15.
26. William Hoffman to Captain Lovell.
27. William Hoffman to the assistant adjutant general.
28. Grosbeck, "Johnston's Army," 3.
29. McDermott, *Frontier Crossroads*, 16.
30. Ibid., 17.
31. H. Ford to commanding officer.
32. Proceedings of the Post Council of Administration.
33. Heth and Morrison, *Memoirs*, 133, 134.
34. Joseph Roberts to commanding officer.
35. S. Cooper to Colonel Monroe.
36. Joseph Roberts to assistant adjutant general.
37. McDermott, *Frontier Crossroads*, 20.
38. Ibid.
39. Ibid.
40. Glass, *Reshaw*, 225.

CHAPTER 2

41. Burton, *City of the Saints*, 141.
42. Ibid.
43. Ibid.
44. Mattes, *Great Platte River Road*, 23.
45. Murray, "Trading Posts," 20.
46. Ibid., 23.
47. Whitehead, "Telegraph and Indians," 4.
48. Ibid.
49. McDermott, *Frontier Crossroads*, 30.
50. Ibid., 31.
51. *Official Roster*, 554.
52. Mokler, *Fort Caspar*, v.

53. Cullimore, *Boys of Company K*, 30.
54. Reid, *Ohio in the War*, 819–21.
55. McDermott, *Frontier Crossroads*, 33.
56. Service, *Life and Letters of Caspar W. Collins*, 5.
57. Ibid., 7.
58. Reid, *Ohio in the War*, 821.
59. McDermott, *Frontier Crossroads*, 34.
60. Spring, *Caspar Collins*, 75.
61. Crawford, *Rekindling Campfires*, 64–65.
62. Vaughn, *Indian Fights*, 8–9.
63. Heaton, "Among the Sioux," 2.
64. *Nebraska Weekly Republican*, "More Indian Atrocities," 1.
65. Hoig, *Sand Creek Massacre*, 145–62.
66. Service, *Life and Letters of Caspar W. Collins*, 9.
67. Ibid., 10.
68. Grinnell, *Fighting Cheyennes*, 185.
69. William Collins to AAAG John Pratt.
70. Mokler, *Fort Caspar*, 1–14.
71. Drew, "Platte Bridge Fight."
72. Spring, *Caspar Collins*, 80.
73. Rea, *Devil's Gate*, 106.
74. *Official Roster*, 567.
75. McDermott, *Frontier Crossroads*, 44.
76. Ibid.
77. Connelley, *Life of Preston B. Plumb*, 195–97.
78. Fairfield, "Eleventh Kansas Regiment," 30–31.
79. Connelley, *Life of Preston B. Plumb*, 195.
80. McDermott, *Frontier Crossroads*, 44.
81. Fairfield, "Eleventh Kansas Regiment," 30.
82. Denison, Kansas State Historical Society.
83. Ibid., 4.
84. Barber, letter to his father, 16.
85. Ibid.
86. Connelley, *Life of Preston B. Plumb*, 196.
87. Cronin, *Casper Mountain*, 33.
88. Connelley, *Life of Preston B. Plumb*, 197–98.
89. Ibid., 197.
90. Connelley, *Life of Preston B. Plumb*, 8.
91. Ibid., 9.

92. Ibid., 210.
93. Ibid., 211.
94. Ibid., 211–12.
95. Ibid., 213.
96. Ibid., 216.
97. Ibid., 218.
98. Ibid., 433.
99. Ibid., 434–35.
100. Ibid.
101. McDermott, *Frontier Crossroads*, 46.
102. Barber, statement of Thomas Barber, 2.
103. McDermott, *Frontier Crossroads*, 47.
104. Ainsworth and Kirkley, *War of the Rebellion*, 442.
105. Palmer, "Powder River Expedition," 64.
106. Coutant, *History of Wyoming and the Far West*, 442.
107. McDermott, *Frontier Crossroads*, 48.
108. Coutant, *History of Wyoming and the Far West*, 442.
109. Johnson, "Hanging of the Chiefs," 60–69.
110. McDermott, *Frontier Crossroads*, 48.
111. Thomas Moonlight to AAAG Price.
112. McDermott, *Frontier Crossroads*, 49.
113. Ainsworth and Kirkley, *War of the Rebellion*, 690.
114. Preston Plumb to AAAG Lieutenant J.J. Taber.
115. McDermott, *Frontier Crossroads*, 49.
116. Connelley, *Life of Preston B. Plumb*, 197–98.
117. Preston B. Plumb to Lieutenant Ira Tabor.
118. Mokler, *Fort Caspar*, 11.
119. McDermott, *Frontier Crossroads*, 50.
120. Thomas Moonlight, Special Order No. 15.
121. McDermott, *Frontier Crossroads*, 52.
122. Pennock, "Diary of Jake Pennock," 10.
123. Ibid., 12.
124. McDermott, *Frontier Crossroads*, 54.
125. Pennock, "Diary of Jake Pennock," 15–16.
126. McDermott, *Frontier Crossroads*, 55.
127. Ibid., 56.
128. Halaas and Masich, *Halfbreed*, 181.

CHAPTER 3

129. Vaughn, *Battle of Platte Bridge*, 58–59.
130. Drew, "Platte Bridge Fight," 1.
131. McDermott, *Frontier Crossroads*, 58.
132. Drew, "Platte Bridge Fight," 1.
133. Vaughn, "Sergeant Custard's Wagon," 277.
134. Cubbison, "Courage, Cowardice, and Discord."
135. Halaas and Masich, *Halfbreed*, 182.
136. Drew, "Platte Bridge Fight," 1.
137. McDermott, *Frontier Crossroads*, 62.
138. Ibid.
139. Walker, "Battle of Platte Bridge," 336.
140. Walker to Wm. E. Connelley, 6.
141. McDermott, *Frontier Crossroads*, 62.
142. Hebard Collection, "The Platte Bridge and Red Buttes Tragedies," University of Wyoming Heritage Center, 15.
143. McDermott, *Frontier Crossroads*, 62.
144. Mokler, *Fort Caspar*, 30–31.
145. Drew, "Platte Bridge Fight," 1.
146. McDermott, *Frontier Crossroads*, 63–64.
147. Pennock, "Diary of Jake Pennock," 131.
148. Halaas and Masich, *Halfbreed*, 183.
149. Mokler, *Fort Caspar*, 32–33.
150. McDermott, *Frontier Crossroads*, 72.
151. Erhardt, "Fight at Platte Bridge," 3.
152. Wilson, "Diary Entry of July 26."
153. Hart, "New Account," 53.
154. Vaughn, *Battle of Platte Bridge*, 70.
155. Walker, "Battle of Platte Bridge," 337.
156. McDermott, *Frontier Crossroads*, 66.
157. Ibid.
158. Drew, "Platte Bridge Fight," 1.
159. McDermott, *Frontier Crossroads*, 69.
160. *Topeka Daily Capital*, "Platte Bridge Fight," 6.
161. Halaas and Masich, *Halfbreed*, 184–85.
162. Coutant, *History of Wyoming from the Earliest Known Discoveries*, 473.
163. Drew, "Platte Bridge Fight," 1.
164. Ibid.

165. Fairfield and Cozzens, *Eyewitnesses to the Indian Wars*, 352–62.
166. *New York Times*, "Indian Troubles."
167. Roenigk, "Reminiscenses of Ferdinand Erhardt."
168. Fairfield and Cozzens, *Eyewitnesses to the Indian Wars*, 352–62.
169. Drew, "Platte Bridge Fight," 1.
170. Pennock, "Diary of Jake Pennock," 133.
171. Crawford, *Kansas in the Sixties*, 266.
172. Pennock, "Diary of Jake Pennock," 133.
173. Maxon Collection, Fort Caspar Museum.
174. Cullimore, *Boys of Company K*, 311.
175. McDermott, *Frontier Crossroads*, 75–76.
176. Walker, "Eleventh Kansas Cavalry," 48.
177. Connelley, *Life of Preston B. Plumb*, 199.
178. McDermott, *Frontier Crossroads*, 79–80.
179. U.S. Returns from Military Posts.
180. George Holliday, *On the Plains in '65*, 86–89.
181. McDermott, *Frontier Crossroads*, 83.
182. Carrington, "Great American Desert," 6.
183. McDermott, *Frontier Crossroads*, 87.
184. Ibid., 91.
185. Ibid.
186. Mokler, "Vern Mokler Related the Following," 186.
187. McDermott, *Frontier Crossroads*, 98.

CONCLUSION

188. Connelley, *Life of Preston B. Plumb*, 199–200.
189. McDermott, *Frontier Crossroads*, 79.
190. Ibid., 108.
191. Kansas State Historical Society, "Martin Anderson."
192. *Highland Weekly News*, "William Collins," 3.
193. Spring, *Caspar Collins*, 96.
194. Mokler, *Fort Caspar*, 61.

BIBLIOGRAPHY

Primary Sources

Unpublished

Fort Caspar Museum
Fort Caspar Museum Collection
Maxon Collection

Kansas State Historical Society
Barber, Thomas. Letter to his father, Kansas State Historical Society, Connelley Papers, Box 6, Book 5, June 8, 1865.
Denison, William. Kansas State Historical Society, Connelley Papers, Box 8, Book 17, 2.
Walker, G.M. Letter to Wm. E. Connelley, Kansas State Historical Society, Box 36, Folder 298, June 1, 1910.

National Archives Letters
William Collins to AAAG John Pratt, February 15, 1865.
S. Cooper to Colonel Monroe, March 23, 1859.
H. Ford to commanding officer at Fort Laramie, April 4, 1859.
William Hoffman to the assistant adjutant general, April 17, 1857.
William Hoffman to Captain A.P. Howe, July 18, 1856.
William Hoffman to Captain Lovell, November 3, 1856.

William Hoffman to Captain Pleasanton, May 24, 1856.
William Hoffman to General Harney, October 10, 1856.
William Hoffman to Henry Heth, May 8, 1856.
William Hoffman to Lieutenant Deshler, October 26, 1855.
William Hoffman to Thomas Twiss, August 9, 1856.
Thomas Moonlight to AAAG Price, May 27, 1865.
Thomas Moonlight to Lieutenant Colonel Preston Plumb, Special Order No. 15, June 14, 1865.
Preston Plumb to AAAG Lieutenant J.J. Taber, June 1, 1865.
Preston B. Plumb to Lieutenant Ira Tabor, June 4, 1865.
Joseph Roberts to assistant adjutant general, April 14, 1859.
Joseph Roberts to commanding officer at Fort Laramie, February 1859.

National Archives Records

Monthly Returns, Post at Platte Bridge, Nebraska Territory, 1855–56.
Proceedings of the Post Council of Administration, Post at Platte Bridge, November 1858–May 1859.
U.S. Returns from Military Posts, October 1865.

Published

Books

Ainsworth, Fred C., and Joseph Kirkley. *The War of the Rebellion: A Compilation of the Official Records of the Union and Confederate Armies*. Vol. 48. Washington, D.C.: Government Printing Office, 1900.
Burton, Richard. *The City of the Saints*. New York: Harper, 1862.
Carrington, Brigadier General Henry. "The Great American Desert and Its Development." *The Hyde Park Historical Record*. Vol. 5. Hyde Park, MA: Hyde Park Historical Society, 1905.
Fairfield, S.H. "The Eleventh Kansas Regiment at Platte Bridge." *Tales of Kansas in the Civil War*. Topeka: Kansas State Historical Society, 2014.
Fairfield, S.H., and Peter Cozzens. *Eyewitnesses to the Indian Wars: 1865–1890*. Vol. 4. Mechanicsburg, PA: Stackpole Books, 2004.
Heth, Henry, and James L. Morrison Jr. *The Memoirs of Henry Heth*. CT, 1974.
Holliday, George. *On the Plains in '65*. N.p., 1883.
Official Roster of the Soldiers of the State of Ohio in the War of the Rebellion. Vol. 9. OH: Werner Printing and Manufacturing, 1887.

Palmer, Henry. "Powder River Expedition." *Civil War Sketches and Incidents*. Vol. 1. Wahoo, NE: Burkley Printing Company, 1902.

Walker, George M. "Battle of Platte Bridge." *Kansas Historical Collection, 1915–1918*. Vol. 14. Topeka: Kansas State Printing Plant, 1918.

———. "Eleventh Kansas Cavalry, 1865, and Battle of Platte Bridge." In *Tales of Kansas in the Civil War*. Kansas State Historical Society. Vol. 14 (1915–18). Tucson, AZ: A Plus Printing Company, 2014.

<u>Magazines</u>

Hart, John. "A New Account of the Battle of Platte Bridge, July 28, 1865: The Recollections of John Benton Hart." *Kansas History* 38, no. 1 (Spring 2015): 53.

Pennock, Jake (Isaac). "Diary of Jake Pennock." *Wyoming Annals* 23, January 1951.

<u>Newspapers</u>

Drew, William. "Platte Bridge Fight." *Osage County Chronicle*, April 20, 1882.

Erhardt, Ferdinand. "Fight at Platte Bridge." *National Tribune*, August 4, 1910.

Heaton, Edward B. "Among the Sioux." *National Tribune*, December 29, 1898.

Highland Weekly News (Hillsboro, OH). "William Collins." November 11, 1880.

Los Angeles Herald. "Preston B. Plumb." December 21, 1891.

Nebraska Weekly Republican. "More Indian Atrocities." August 23, 1865.

New York Times. "Indian Troubles: A Fight in the Platte County." July 29, 1865.

Whitehead, Charles. "The Telegraph and Indians." *Forest Republican* (PA), September 28, 1881.

Wilson, Jean. "Diary Entry of July 26." *Leavenworth Daily Times*, August 30, 1865.

SECONDARY SOURCES

Books

Barnes, Jeff. *Forts of the Northern Plains: Guide to Historic Military Posts of the Plains Indian Wars*. Mechanicsburg, PA: Stackpole Books, 2008.

Connelley, William Elsey. *The Life of Preston B. Plumb, 1837–1891: United States Senator from Kansas*. Chicago: Browne & Howell Company, 1913.

Coutant, C.G. *History of Wyoming and the Far West*. New York: Hudson Book Company, 1899.

———. *The History of Wyoming from the Earliest Known Discoveries in Three Volumes*. Vol. 1. Laramie, WY: Chaplin, Spafford & Mathison, Printers, 1899.

Bibliography

Crawford, Lewis F. *Rekindling Campfires: The Exploits of Ben Arnold*. ND: Capital Publishing, 1926.

Crawford, Samuel. *Kansas in the Sixties*. Chicago: W.F. Hall Printing Company, 1911.

Cronin, Vaughn Stephen. *Casper Mountain: The Magic Yesterday and Today*. Casper, WY: Vaughn's Publishing, 1998.

Cullimore, Lee M. *The Boys of Company K*. Glendo, WY: High Plains Press, 2012.

Frazer, Robert W. *Forts of the West: An Indispensible Handbook of All Presidios and Military Forts West of the Mississippi Up to 1898*. Norman: University of Oklahoma Press, 1965.

Glass, Jefferson. *Reshaw: The Life and Times of John Baptiste Richard*. Glendo, WY: High Plains Press, 2014.

Grace Raymond Hebard Collection. "The Platte Bridge and Red Buttes Tragedies." University of Wyoming Heritage Center.

Grinnell, George Bird. *The Fighting Cheyennes*. New York: Charles Scribner's Sons, 1915.

Halaas, David Fridtjof, and Andrew E. Masich. *Halfbreed: The Remarkable True Story of George Bent: Caught Between the Worlds of the Indian and the White Man*. Boston: Da Capo Press, 2004.

Hoig, Stan. *The Sand Creek Massacre*. Norman: University of Oklahoma Press, 1961.

Mattes, Merrill J. *The Great Platte River Road: The Covered Wagon Mainline via Fort Kearny to Fort Laramie*. Lincoln: University of Nebraska Press, 1987.

McDermott, John D. *Frontier Crossroads: The History of Fort Caspar and the Upper Platte Crossing*. Casper, WY: City of Casper, 1997.

Mokler, Alfred James. *Fort Caspar*. Casper, WY: Mountain States Lithographing, 1939.

Rea, Tom. *Devil's Gate: Owning the Land, Owning the Story*. Norman: University of Oklahoma Press, 2006.

Reid, Whitelaw. *Ohio in the War: Her Statesmen, Generals, and Soldiers*. Vol. II. Cincinnati, OH: Moore, Wilstach & Baldwin, 1868.

Service, Alex. *The Life and Letters of Caspar W. Collins*. Casper, WY: City of Casper, 2000.

Spring, Agnes Wright. *Caspar Collins: The Life and Exploits of an Indian Fighter of the Sixties*. Lincoln: University of Nebraska Press, 1969.

Vaughn, J.W. *The Battle of Platte Bridge*. Norman: University of Oklahoma Press, 1963.

———. *Indian Fights: New Facts on Seven Encounters*. Norman: University of Oklahoma Press, 1966.

Magazines

Johnson, Dorothy M. "The Hanging of the Chiefs." *Montana: The Magazine of Western History* 20, no. 3 (1970).

Mokler, Vern. "Vern Mokler Related the Following Exciting Story of Caspar Collins and Other Events at Fort Caspar." *Annals of Wyoming Volume* 28 (April 1956).

Murray, Robert A. "Trading Posts, Forts and Bridges of the Casper Area—Unraveling the Tangle on the Upper Platte." *Annals of Wyoming* (Spring 1975).

Vaughn, J.W. "Sergeant Custard's Wagon." *Annals of Wyoming* 32 (April 1960).

Newspapers

Cubbison, Douglas R. "Courage, Cowardice, and Discord at Platte Bridge Station." *Casper Journal*, July 10, 2014. casperjournal.com/news/article_c8b6b19c-6a38-5874-95ad-3a3b105c2960.html.

Grosbeck, Kathryn. "Johnston's Army Turned Out to Be Financial Blessing to Mormons." *Provo Daily Herald*, February 20, 1967.

Hemman, Ray. "Broken Promises, Wars Ended Indians' Reign." *Hutchinson News*, June 25, 1986.

Topeka Daily Capital. "The Platte Bridge Fight." July 3, 1882, 6.

Websites

The Church of Jesus Christ of Latter Day Saints. "Upper Platte (Mormon) Ferry." history.lds.org/place/pioneer-story-upper-platte-mormon-ferry?lang=eng.

Kansas State Historical Society. "Martin Anderson." www.kansasmemory.org/item/223915.

Roenigk, Adolph. "Reminiscenses of Ferdinand Erhardt." In *Pioneer History of Kansas* (n.p., n.d.). www.kancoll.org/books/roenigk/chpt6.htm.

INDEX

M

P

R

S

T

ABOUT THE AUTHOR

Johanna Wickman has lived in Casper for over twenty years. She holds AA degrees in German and museum and gallery studies from Casper College and a BA in humanities and fine arts from the University of Wyoming and completed her master's degree in history in 2014 at the University of Nebraska–Kearney.

Wickman presided as a museum director in the area of Palm Springs, California, from 2009 through 2011. While there, she increased museum attendance from 300 visitors per month (February 2010) to more than 2,900 guests in February 2011 through a combination of spectacular exhibits and programs.

While in California, she was a founding board member of the Desert Cities Museum Association and the Coachella Valley Emergency Preparedness Network for museums and was a featured panelist at the 2011 California Association of Museums conference. Recently, she served on the planning committee for the 150th anniversary of the Battle of Platte Bridge and Caspar Collins Days held in July 2015 at Fort Caspar.

She was elected to the board of the Fort Caspar Museum Association in October 2015.

Currently, Wickman is the president of two companies working with museums. Wickman Historical Consultants offers historical research services and is under contract with the State of Wyoming Military Department at the Wyoming Veterans Museum in Casper. Her second company, Creative Museum Solutions, works with museums and historical societies to offer exhibit design services, marketing services, collections care, gift shop management and myriad other assistance related to museums. Recently, she created the website Network-Museums.com as a central hub for museum staff nationwide to interact with each other and offer valuable information and resources.

ABOUT THE FOREWORD AUTHOR

Douglas R. Cubbison holds a BA in history from Indiana University of Pennsylvania. He has served for over ten years active and reserve duty as a U.S. Army field artillery officer and deployed to Afghanistan in 2007 in support of Operation Enduring Freedom as the command historian for CJTF-76. Cubbison has previously served as a military historian with the U.S. Army Combat Studies Institute at Fort Leavenworth, Kansas; as command historian with the 10th Mountain Division and Fort Drum, New York; and as cultural resources manager at the U.S. Military Academy, West Point, New York. As a captain in the U.S. Army, Cubbison was awarded a U.S. Army Commendation Medal (ARCOM) for his establishment of an Officers Professional Development (OPD) course, focused on using military history to develop leadership skills, while with the 1st Squadron, 4th Cavalry with the 1st Infantry Division. This OPD program was recognized as being the best in the division. In 1990, Captain Cubbison was awarded another ARCOM for his use of military history as a training tool with the 3392nd USARF School. Cubbison was also awarded a Civilian Achievement Medal by West Point for establishing a consultation program and relationship between West Point and the Stockbridge Munsee Band of Mohican Indians.

Cubbison is a widely published professional military historian, with nine books on various military history subjects and one historic novel. His published books are *Barksdale: The Man, the Base*; *"The Artillery Never Gained More Honour": The British Artillery in the 1776 Valcour Island and 1777 Saratoga Campaigns*; *The American Northern Theater Army in 1776: The Ruin and Reconstruction of the Continental Force*; *The British Defeat of the French in Pennsylvania in 1758: A Military History of the Forbes Campaign against Fort Duquesne*; *Wanat: Combat Action in Afghanistan, 2008*; *Burgoyne and the Saratoga Campaign: His Papers*; *"All Canada in the Hands of the British": General Jeffery Amherst and the 1760 Campaign to Conquer Canada*; *Adventures of the Green Cloth* (historic novel); *On Campaign Against Fort Duquesne: The Braddock and Forbes Expeditions, 1755–1758, through the Experiences of Quartermaster Sir John St. Clair*; and *Sallie: A Regiment and Its Dog in the Civil War*.

Cubbison is currently the curator for the Wyoming Veterans Memorial Museum in Casper, Wyoming. He is the sheriff of the Casper Posse of Westerners International. He serves on the board for the Fort Caspar Museum Association and on the executive board of the Wyoming State Historical Society. He is currently working on his next history, on the role of the U.S. Army in Wyoming and Montana during the Indian Wars period.